DATE DUE

MOSES

The Man and his Vision

David Daiches

PRAEGER PUBLISHERS
New York

Published in the United States of America in 1975
by Praeger Publishers, Inc.
111 Fourth Avenue, New York, N.Y. 10003

Library of Congress Cataloging in Publication Data
Daiches, David, 1912–
Moses, the man and his vision.

Includes index.
1. Moses. I. Title.
BS580.M6D3   222'.1'0924[B]   74-11918
ISBN 0-275-33740-5

Printed in Great Britain

Contents

To Chaim Raphael
'the onlie begetter'

Author's note

All biblical quotations, unless otherwise specified, have been taken from the Authorized Version.

I

Hebrews in Egypt

If it were not for the Bible we should know nothing of Moses. He is not mentioned anywhere else. He first appears in the second chapter of Exodus and the story of his life and achievements is told intermittently there and in the three subsequent biblical books until we are told of his death in the last chapter of Deuteronomy. Later biblical references to Moses refer back to the story as told in these three books. The biblical account of Moses is not history as we understand it: it represents the coming together of a variety of traditions, many at first handed down orally, relating to the sense of their own past and of their special relationship to God and to their land developed and solemnly remembered by the people of Israel. It includes elements of myth and ritual, symbolic situations, the repetition of the same or similar incidents in an attempt not to discard any of the traditions which testified to them, conflation of different incidents into one in order to emphasize the clear pattern of Israel's history, the placing of the story of Israel's deliverance from slavery in Egypt as part of an unfolding of a divinely appointed destiny going back to God's promise to the Patriarchs, passages of ancient poetry celebrating and glorifying moments in Israel's history, and numerous other features that no historian could accept as legitimate. Yet the history underlying it is real; Moses was a real person; the exodus from Egypt and the entry into the Promised Land were real events; and the religious experience that the Bible tells us

9

Hazor, in upper Galilee, the city destroyed by Joshua in the late 13th century BC. The famous Hebrew archaeologist Y. Yadin has carried out extensive excavations there.

Moses first underwent alone with his flock of sheep in the wilderness of Midian was a genuine experience undergone by the man who remoulded the religious consciousness of his people and in doing so made possible the history of both Judaism and Christianity.

How can we know this? Our knowledge comes from putting together information provided by archaeologists, ancient historians, linguists, anthropologists and students of comparative religion with the results of textual study of the biblical story and the evidence such a study provides of the nature and development of Israel's traditions about her own history. We now know a great deal about conditions in Egypt at the time when we can show that the events remembered in Exodus took place; we also know a great deal about conditions in Mesopotamia and Palestine at that time and about the relations – cultural, social, political, economic – between Semitic peoples

Palestine and Mesopotamia in the time of the Patriarchs

and Egyptians. We can construct with considerable accuracy the whole context of Moses' life. And even if in some degree Moses' existence as a person whose acts and experiences correspond to the traditions about him preserved in the Bible remains a matter of inference and conjecture, the inferences and conjectures derive from information solid enough to enable us to construct some kind of picture of Moses and his life's work. Thus although a history of Moses is bound to be 'conjectural history' (to use a phrase invented by Dugald Stewart), it need not be pure speculation.

The account of Israel's slavery in Egypt, with which Exodus begins, is presented as part of a continuing story which goes back to the Patriarchs in Genesis. The story really opens with God's call to Abraham to leave Haran (in north-western Mesopotamia) and migrate south-eastwards to the country later known as Palestine: 'Get thee out of thy country, and from thy kindred, and from thy father's house, unto a land that I will show thee. And I will make of thee a great nation, and I will bless thee, and make thy name great; and thou shalt be a blessing' (12: 1–2). So Abraham and his family migrated to Palestine (Canaan), then moved on southwards to Egypt to dwell there for a while 'for there was famine in the land'. Then he returned to Palestine, 'very rich in cattle, in silver, and in gold', and dwelt 'in the plain of Mamre the Amorite'. God renewed his promise to Abraham, and his wife bore him a son in old age. The beginning of Chapter 20 of Genesis tells us that 'Abraham journeyed . . . toward the south country, and dwelt between Kadesh and Shur, and sojourned in Gerar'. (This has been rendered by W. F. Albright, liveliest of modern biblical scholars, as: 'And Abraham departed . . . to the Negeb, keeping between Kadesh and the Wall [of Egypt], while he was a resident alien at Gerar.')

Abraham's son was Isaac, whom his father sent back to his own native Mesopotamia for a wife. Later Isaac dwelt at Gerar and the Lord appeared to him and renewed the promise he had made to Abraham. Isaac's marginally younger son Jacob (whose name was later symbolically changed to Israel) was conscious of his father's and grandfather's special relationship to God, and manoeuvred to have for himself the birthright that would normally belong to the elder brother, so that he could carry on the divine mission. Jacob too was sent out of Canaan back to his grandfather's original home of Haran to find a wife, and on the journey there he had his own special encounter with God. In fact he got two wives, his cousin Leah and her younger sister Rachel, since his uncle would not let him have the younger without taking the elder first. But it was Rachel whom he loved, and it was Rachel who bore the two youngest of his twelve sons, Joseph and Benjamin. The jealousy of the elder brothers led

OVERLEAF *The Departure of Abraham*, a painting after J. Bassano.

11

Abraham journeying into the land of Canaan, by Gustave Doré.

to Joseph's being sold as a slave into Egypt, and there, as a result of his own remarkable powers and of divine purpose, he rose to be Pharaoh's vizier. When famine in Canaan forced Jacob to send his sons into Egypt to buy corn, on two separate occasions, they met the now mighty and powerful Joseph, whom they did not recognize but who recognized them. Eventually Joseph forgave his brothers for what they had done to him and persuaded Pharaoh to invite them and his father to settle in that part of Egypt called Goshen. This they did, and prospered in Goshen. And Jacob died, and eventually Joseph too died, first saying to his brethren: 'I die; and God will surely visit you, and bring you out of this land unto the land which he sware to Abraham, to Isaac, and to Jacob. And Joseph took an oath of the children of Israel, saying, God will surely visit you, and ye shall carry up my bones from hence.'

Exodus opens with an account of Jacob's descendants, the children of Israel, prospering and multiplying in Egypt. Then 'there arose a new king over Egypt, which knew not Joseph'. He was afraid that this alien people in his country would grow too powerful, so he enslaved them and made other arrangements for weakening them. 'And they built for Pharaoh treasure cities,

Joseph, left by his brothers in an empty well, is sold by passing Midianite merchants to a caravan of Ishmaelites: by Raphael.

Pithom and Raamses.' Pharaoh ordered the two Hebrew midwives, called Shiphrah and Puah, to kill all male Hebrews. (Why Hebrews at this point, and not Israelites? The term, as we shall see, is of the greatest significance.) The midwives, however, found an excuse not to do this. The Israelites continued to multiply. Pharaoh then ordered that all male Israelite babies should be cast into the river. And it is at this point that Moses first appears on the scene.

What are we to make of all this? Who was Abraham and why and when did he leave Haran for Palestine? What were the Patriarchs doing wandering up and down Canaan and in and out of Egypt? How could the great Pharaoh (king) of Egypt appoint an alien former slave to be, after himself, the most powerful person in the land? And how did he come to invite a mass of Israelites to settle in one of the most fertile regions of Lower Egypt? And why did a later Pharaoh turn against them? We must try to answer these questions if we want to set the stage properly for Moses.

There is now abundant archaeological evidence that between the twenty-third and twentieth centuries BC nomadic invaders caused considerable disruption in the life of Palestine: cities were destroyed, sometimes with apparent suddenness and violence. The destroyed cities were not at first rebuilt by the invaders, who probably continued their semi-nomadic way of life. Eventually they did settle down in villages, but the evidence suggests that their buildings were crude compared with those they had destroyed. Who were they? We do not know what they called themselves, but we do possess solid reasons for believing that they were a North-west Semitic people from Mesopotamia and Syria, referred to as 'Amorites' (i.e. 'westerners') by their neighbours. Archaeological and epigraphical discoveries in the Mesopotamian centre of Mari (on the west bank of the Euphrates, some fifteen miles north of the modern border between Syria and Iraq) have revealed a great deal about the society, institutions and customs of the West Semitic tribes in the third millennium BC, while the fifteenth-century BC tablets found in the excavations at Nuzi (in north-eastern Iraq) throw a vivid light on the customs of the Hurrians (whom the Bible calls Horites), from whose political and religious centre Haran (a city in the middle Euphrates valley) Abraham migrated to Palestine. Many of the activities of Abraham, Isaac and Jacob as recorded in Genesis make sense only in the light of Hurrian procedures and practices revealed in the Nuzi tablets and confirm the biblical story of Abraham's having come from Haran and maintaining contact with it after he had left. (Esau's sale of his birthright to Jacob and Abraham's and Isaac's claiming that their wives were their sisters when visiting foreign potentates are among the otherwise puzzling features of the biblical story which become clear as soon as we see them as representing echoes of the Patriarchs' Mesopotamian origins recorded in Palestine in a later age by those who no longer fully understood the meaning of the customs they were describing.)

In addition to the Mari and the Nuzi texts, we have other material illustrating the nature of the world out of which the Patriarchs emerged and into which they moved: it includes the 450 clay tablets found at the ancient city of Alalakh (now Tell el-Atchana, in Turkey), written in Akkadian (a group of East Semitic dialects which became the *lingua franca* of the ancient Middle East), some dating from the eighteenth century BC and some from the fifteenth, illustrating the social, economic and political life of the city; the Ras Shamra tablets from Ugarit (about seven miles north of Latakia), dating from the fourteenth century but containing much earlier material; and the so-called Execration Texts dating from about the end of the Middle Kingdom of Egypt (eighteenth century BC) which record the real or potential enemies of the country as well as listing the lands and territories adjacent to Egypt. Then there are the fourteenth century BC Tell el-Amarna letters – cuneiform tablets in Akkadian, except for two in Hurrian and one in Hittite – which vividly

ABOVE Joseph's men find his silver cup in Benjamin's sack: from a 16th-century misericord in Amiens Cathedral. BELOW Joseph as overseer of Pharaoh's granaries: after Alma-Tadema.

reveal the relation between the Egyptian government and the confused and turbulent rulers of their precariously subject cities of Palestine. One could go on listing further important archaeological finds, but our interest lies less in listing sources than in clarifying what they tell us about the historical background of Israel in Egypt.

The biblical picture of the Patriarchs wandering in Palestine between the hill country and the desert Negeb, maintaining contact with their ancestral Mesopotamia and also moving south to Egypt when food became scarce, confirms what we can now deduce from the sources just referred to: they were nomads, or semi-nomads, travelling regularly with their donkeys and their caravans (for they were ass-nomads, not camel-nomads: the camel was not effectively domesticated until between the fifteenth and thirteenth centuries BC in Arabia, and references to camels in Genesis appear to be later picturesque additions to the original traditions). They travelled the caravan routes between Mesopotamia and Egypt in the Middle Bronze Age – the first part of the second millennium BC. They did not refer to themselves as 'Hebrews', but they are referred to as Hebrews by others (see Genesis 14: 13, which is clearly an outside view of Abraham, who suddenly appears as a prosperous clan chief who can mobilize his own army at short notice). This word 'Hebrew' (*'Ibri*) is now thought to be related to a similar-sounding word which appears in a variety of forms throughout documents of the ancient Middle East. The Egyptians transcribed it as *'a-pi-ru*, or (since Egyptian hieroglyphic script can be written only in consonants) *'pr.w*, or simply *'pr*. It is *Habiru* or *Hapiru* in Akkadian cuneiform. The Amarna letters refer frequently to the 'Apiru (also sometimes referred to as SA.GAZ) as making trouble. An administrative letter of the time of the Pharaoh Ramesses II refers to providing corn for the *'pr* who were drawing stones for the great gateway of one of the buildings of Raamses. Who were these Hebrew, 'Apiru, Habiru people? The word appears not to be the name of a race or a nation, but of a class of people who worked the caravan routes of the Middle East; the word probably means something like donkey-men or caravan-men, perhaps originally dusty men (the Hebrew for dust is *'afar*, and Hebrew *f* and *p* are closely related). They travelled and traded with their families and their flocks and herds, never settling for very long in one place. They operated sometimes as smiths and traded among other things in musical instruments. (Cf. Genesis 4: 20–2: 'And Adah bare Jabal: he was the father of such as dwell in tents, and of such as have cattle. And his brother's name was Jubal: he was the father of all such as handle the harp and the organ. And Zillah she also bare Tubal-cain, and instructor of

A view of the Negeb desert.

19

every artificer in brass and iron.') The Patriarchs appear to have been this sort of people, though of course the term 'Apiru referred to a much larger class of people, to a heterogeneous band of stateless wanderers who sometimes posed a threat to settled cities and civilizations. So the ancient Israelites were 'Apiru, though far from all 'Apiru were Israelites. As for the name 'Israel', we cannot be certain of its origin and meaning (the etymology given in Genesis when Jacob's name is changed to Israel being, like many such biblical explanations, folk etymology only). The name is first found outside the Bible in the stele (upright slab bearing inscriptions) of the Pharaoh Merneptah (1219 BC). By this time the term 'Israel' had replaced the term 'Hebrew' just as other 'Apiru or Habiru groups, as they settled down in territories they had conquered or in whose population they had become absorbed, acquired new national names. The term disappears in sources outside the Bible at about the same time as it ceased to be used in the Bible.

The patriarchal period, the age of Abraham, Isaac and Jacob and their semi-nomadic wanderings, cannot be more specifically dated than the first half of the second millennium BC, say 1950 to 1800 BC, in the Middle Bronze Age. In the light of modern knowledge we can see these biblical characters, if not clearly as individuals attested by other sources (for there is no certain mention of any of the Patriarchs in contemporary inscriptions), then as clan leaders, or perhaps as each character representing a whole clan, living and working in a recognizable context. When some of them settled in Egypt the context changes. In Egyptian history this is the time of the Twelfth Dynasty (c. 1991–1786 BC), during which, as is shown by Egyptian records and excavations in Gezer and Megiddo in Palestine, Biblus, Qatna and Ugarit in Lebanon and Syria, and other sources, Egypt ruled, with varying degrees of firmness, Palestine, Phoenicia and southern Syria, and trade between Egypt and these countries flourished. A well-known painting in the tomb of Prince Khnumhotep III at Beni Hasan in Middle Egypt (c. 1890 BC) shows the arrival at Khnumhotep's court of a trading caravan of thirty-seven brightly dressed travelling Semitic smiths and musicians, thus nicely illustrating the verses already quoted from Genesis 4 about Jabal and Tubal-cain. At the beginning of the Twelfth Dynasty the capital was moved from Thebes to Memphis. During the period of this dynasty the god Amun took on a new and dominating importance, becoming identified with Re' as Amun-Re'. Canals were dug, forts were built, copper mines were worked and foreign trade flourished. Medicine and mathematics flourished too, and this was the Golden Age of Egyptian literature.

The Middle Kingdom of Egypt collapsed about 1786 BC in chaos and civil war. When the smoke clears, about the end of the eighteenth century, we find

ABOVE Statue of Ramesses II at the temple of Abu Simbel. BELOW Ramesses' charioteers at the battle of Karnak: from an Egyptian bas-relief.

LEFT Basalt stele found at Bethshean: Ramesses (right) and the god Amun-Re (left).

RIGHT The Temple of Amun at Karnak. BELOW View of Ramesses' temple to Amun at Thebes.

the Hyksos in control of the country. These appear to be a mixture of Semites and Hurrians (the name Hyksos, *hekau khoswe*, means 'rulers of foreign lands') who began by infiltrating into the Eastern Delta as traders and herdsmen and eventually seized power in the confusions and civil war of the Egyptian Thirteenth Dynasty. They established control of the Nile Valley as far south as Hermopolis, and claimed, though never fully exercised, overlordship of all Upper Egypt as well. They established their capital at Avaris, which they fortified in a sophisticated manner. They introduced the horse and chariot into Egypt – a permanent legacy, as we shall see in looking at the Egyptian pursuit of the Israelites after the exodus – or at least we first find the horse-drawn chariot in Egypt during the Hyksos period. Though the Hyksos assimilated Egyptian culture readily they were bitterly resented by the Egyptians, and when they were finally expelled in about 1550 after a war of liberation begun by the Egyptian rulers of Thebes, to be replaced by the rulers of the Eighteenth Dynasty (*c.* 1570–1305 BC), the Egyptians always regarded them as vicious outsiders and the memory of their rule was preserved in shame and hatred.

The Hyksos and the Hebrews were racially akin. Some of the Hyksos rulers had Semitic names: one, for example, was called Jacob-el (*Ya'qub-'al*), 'May El give protection', and another, Jacob-baal, 'May Baal protect'. Most scholars now agree that there is some connection between the Hyksos rule of Egypt and the settling of the Hebrews there. It seems reasonable to assume that the Hyksos, who themselves had travelled the caravan routes to Egypt for centuries before they finally took power there, favoured other 'Apiru groups and encouraged them to settle. When the Pharaoh Amosis (*c.* 1552–1527) captured Avaris and expelled the Hyksos from Egypt, pursuing them to Palestine and opening the way to Asia and so to the great age of the Egyptian empire in the Eighteenth and Nineteenth Dynasties (the New Kingdom), the Hebrews in Egypt were left without protectors. Contemporary documents show that the Hyksos who escaped slaughter were enslaved. It is reasonable to suppose that the Hebrews, now unprotected by the Establishment, were also enslaved at this time. This would place Joseph's rise to power under the Hyksos and make Amosis the Pharaoh who 'knew not Joseph'.

All this fits in with much of both the biblical and the archaeological evidence, although the Bible account is not always consistent and there are some teasing problems of chronology. Again we must remember that the Bible is not presented as history in the modern sense, but as the traditions of a people about their national and religious origins, containing a considerable element of what German scholars call *Heilsgeschichte*, sacral history ('sacral: of or pertaining to sacred rites and observances'). The biblical narrative includes stories and traditions handed down as saga, and saga represents the imagination of a people working on a sense of its own past. That ancestors of the people of Israel served as slaves in Egypt cannot be doubted: no people would invent for themselves such a shameful episode in their history. That they were eventually liberated and led out by a charismatic leader cannot be doubted either. The liberation and the character of its leader were most solemnly engraved on the national memory. We may if we wish add to this the evidence of Egyptian names in early Israelite history – that of Moses himself, as we shall see; Merari, son of Levi (Genesis 46:11); Phinehas, grandson of Aaron (Exodus 6:25) and others; the evidence of the large number of Semitic words that entered the Egyptian language and the intermingling of Canaanite and Egyptian traditions about gods; references to 'Apiru in Egyptian texts first as captives and then frequently as slaves; and the names of the specific cities the Hebrew slaves worked on according to Exodus, Pithom and Raamses. (Raamses was in fact the old Hyksos capital of Avaris rebuilt and again made the capital by Sethos I [c. 1305–1290 BC] and his successor Ramesses II [c. 1290–1224]. Ramesses called the rebuilt city Per-Ra'mses, the House of Ramesses. Pithom, in Egyptian Per-'Itm, House of Atum, was on the site of the present hill ruin Tell er-Retabeh in the eastern Nile Delta west of Lake Timsah.) Another interesting piece of evidence is the names of the two Hebrew midwives mentioned in Exodus 1:15, Shiphrah and Puah: these have been shown to be common North-west Semitic names in the second millennium BC and not, as was once believed, invented decorative Hebrew names chosen for their pretty meaning ('Beauty' and 'Splendour' respectively).

Scholars differ on how to interpret some of the chronological problems, but the general position attested by modern scholarship can be briefly stated. (Some details of the argument follow this summary of the general position, but they may be omitted if the reader's main interest is in the conclusions rather than in the balancing of conjectures and probabilities.) Ancestors of the Israelites entered Egypt at different times in the Hyksos period, while varieties of 'Apiru also came there or were brought there at different times. The Bible story of the settling of Jacob and his clan in Egypt is a conflation or telescoping of a fairly lengthy and complex process. The story of Joseph's rise to power reflects a historical truth about at least one Semitic vizier in Egypt. Many ancestors of the Israelites (we must remember that there was as yet no 'people of Israel': that was in large measure the creation of Moses) remained in Palestine; others entered and left Egypt voluntarily; other 'Apiru were taken there as prisoners of war; and others again, Hebrews or 'Apiru or proto-Israelites, settled there. Hebrews were certainly slaves in Egypt under Sethos I and Ramesses II, and if they were enslaved under Amosis 250 years earlier, immediately after the expulsion of the Hyksos, then either later Israelite

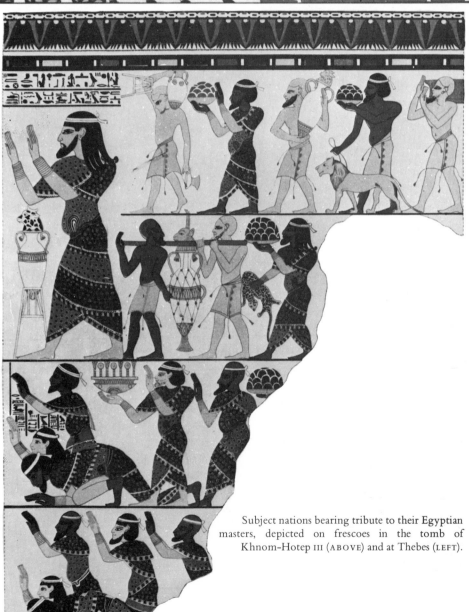

Subject nations bearing tribute to their Egyptian masters, depicted on frescoes in the tomb of Khnom-Hotep III (ABOVE) and at Thebes (LEFT).

ABOVE Akhenaten with Nefertiti in the rays of the Sun God: from Amarna. BELOW, LEFT Stone head of Akhenaten. RIGHT Young man, possibly related to Akhenaten, depicted on a stele at Amarna.

tradition telescoped the period between Amosis and Sethos, regarding the latter as the first enslaver of the children of Israel and his successor Ramesses II as the Pharaoh of the exodus, or there was more than one separate period of enslavement.

What leads us to accept this general picture? And why cannot we be more specific? We can look only at some part of the evidence, but this will at least illustrate the nature of the problem. In Exodus 12: 40 we are told that the length of the Israelite sojourn in Egypt was 430 years. If, as most scholars think, the exodus from Egypt took place in the reign of Ramesses II, then it was most likely to have taken place between 1280 and 1250 BC. Four hundred and thirty years back bring us to 1700 BC, which is when the Hyksos established themselves. In 1 Kings 6: 1 we are told that King Solomon (who reigned during the second third of the tenth century BC) began to build the Temple 'in the four hundred and eightieth year after the children of Israel were come out of the land of Egypt', and this if taken literally would put the exodus at about 1450–1430. A few scholars accept this date for the exodus, though the majority prefer the later date. If we interpret the 480 years of 1 Kings as meaning 12 generations – and we know that 40 years was the symbolic biblical period for a generation, as is suggested by Numbers 32: 13 and Psalms 95: 10 – and reduce the symbolic figure of 40 to the more realistic figure of 25 years for a generation, this reduces the period from 480 years to 300 years, which would put the exodus at about 1270 BC, 300 years after the end of the Egyptian war of liberation against the Hyksos and the establishment of the New Kingdom.

In Genesis 15: 13–16 God tells Abraham that his seed 'shall be a stranger in a land that is not theirs, and shall serve them; and they shall afflict them four hundred years. . . . But in the fourth generation they shall come hither [i.e. back to Palestine] again.' In Exodus 12: 40 we are told that 'the sojourning of the children of Israel, who dwelt in Egypt, was four hundred and thirty years'. Again, according to Exodus 6: 16–20, Moses was a great-grandson of Levi, Joseph's brother (and son of Jacob), while Numbers 26: 50 tells us that Moses' mother Jochebed was the daughter of Levi; this agrees with Exodus 6: 20, which says that Jochebed was the sister of Amram, Moses' father, and so Moses' aunt. So there are biblical traditions giving the stay of the Israelites in Egypt as anything from 430 years to 3 generations (which in biblical terms is somewhat over 100 years). It is significant that Genesis 15 puts side by side a period of 400 years and a period of 4 generations as representing the same length of time. It looks as though different traditions have been preserved, referring presumably to different aspects of Hebrew experience in Egypt. Further, the phrase 'they shall come hither again' in Genesis 15: 16 suggests that this was written from the point of view of people living in Palestine. This supports archaeological evidence that some Hebrews remained in Palestine and never settled in Egypt at all, and that these were later joined in an association with a common religious and historical tradition with those who had escaped from Egypt in the solemn assembly of the tribes at Shechem called by Joshua after the re-entry into the Promised Land (Joshua 24).

If we accept the Hyksos period as being the period during which Joseph rose to power, as seems highly plausible in view of the situation described above, what are we to make of the evidence, accepted by some scholars, that Joseph's Pharaoh was the very much later Akhenaten (*c.* 1364–1347)? Akhenaten, who changed his name from Amenophis IV, came out against the Egyptian worship of the high god Amun and substituted the worship of Aten, the round disc of the sun, whom he declared to be the sole god. (The name Akhenaten, which he adopted, means 'Splendour of Aten'.) Akhenaten's break with the Theban priesthood in establishing Aten worship – which, it is worth noting, was a species of monotheism – was fiercely repudiated after his death as representing a vicious heresy. In looking for holders of high office to replace the ousted members of the Theban priesthood, who had traditionally filled the top government posts, might he not have turned to some of the Semitic immigrants we know to have been in the country and found his Joseph among them? The Tell el-Amarna letters, which date from the reign of Akhenaten and his father Amenophis III, include apparently unanswered appeals to the Egyptian government for help against 'Apiru attackers. If Joseph was Akhenaten's vizier, might he not, recognizing a kinship between Hebrew and 'Apiru, have been responsible for preventing or holding up Egyptian assistance to those the 'Apiru were attacking? This view would be consistent with the position taken by some scholars that Joseph lived long after the Hyksos period, though they concede that there were earlier Semites in Egypt, one of whom may well have risen to a high position. Then there is the mention in the Harris papyrus (1215–1209 BC) of Arisu, a Syrian administrator in Egypt, who seems to represent a close parallel to the case of Joseph. If Arisu is Joseph we must set the exodus very late, perhaps in about 1130 BC. This is inconsistent with other evidence. We know that some 'Apiru were still in Egypt long after the exodus, for there are contemporary references to them in Egyptian sources, and Arisu may have been one of those.

The stele of Merneptah of 1219 BC refers in grandiloquent terms to the defeat by Egyptian forces of a number of peoples, including Israel:

> Israel is desolated, his seed is not;
> Palestine is become a widow for Egypt.

Now we do not have to take this literally, for Egyptian records never admit any Egyptian defeat and frequently describe defeats as victories. But it is evidence of an engagement with Israel in Palestine. It is conceivable that it is a reference to the pursuit of the escaping Israelites, in which case the Pharaoh of the exodus would be Merneptah (*c.* 1224–1211), but this is unlikely. It is much more likely that this is a reference to Israelites settled in Palestine after the exodus (they were never called Israelites in Palestine before the exodus). This is consistent with a date of about 1270 BC for the exodus and with the biblical period of a generation in the wilderness before entry into Palestine. Recently discovered archaeological evidence shows that the Palestinian city of Hazor – destroyed by fire by the invading Israelites under Joshua (Joshua 11: 10–13) – was destroyed in the latter part of the thirteenth century, which confirms this date.

In any case, weighing all the biblical and extra-biblical evidence, we can be certain that different traditions about the Israelite experience in Egypt were long handed down before they were put together in the Bible and that these represented a more complex set of events than appears in the biblical account. We can also be reasonably certain that by the end of the thirteenth century BC the Israelites – now really the people of Israel – were settled in parts at least of Palestine, and the Egyptian experience was finally behind them, though never to be forgotten. We must now turn to look at the part played by Moses in all this.

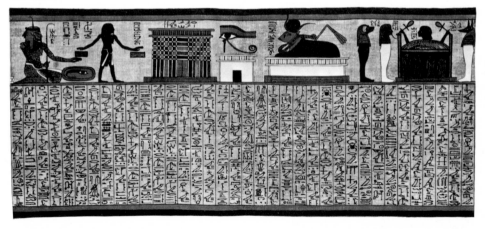

Facsimile of *The Book of the Dead* illustrating scenes of the after-life looked forward to by the Egyptians.

2

The Call in the Wilderness

'Now these are the names of the children of Israel, which came unto Egypt.' So Exodus begins, with a reference to the children of Israel in the literal sense of the sons of Israel (Jacob's other name). But when in verse 7 of the opening chapter we read, 'And the children of Israel were fruitful, and increased abundantly, and multiplied, and waxed exceeding mighty; and the land was filled with them', we see the beginning of an important new use of the phrase. 'The children of Israel' now and henceforth means the Israelites, the people of Israel, retroactively given unity as a people in the light of subsequent events. Exodus goes on to tell how these people now become the object of divine attention and the beneficiaries of divine action.

But first comes their enslavement. The Bible reports this in what Martin Buber has described as 'an exalted poetic tone'. It has the rhythms of orally transmitted saga, which can be heard even in English translation:

> But the more they afflicted them, the more they multiplied and grew.
> And they were grieved because of the children of Israel.
> And the Egyptians made the children of Israel to serve with rigour:
> And they made their lives bitter with hard bondage, in mortar, and in
> brick, and in all manner of service in the field: all the service,
> wherein they made them serve, was with rigour.

Slavery was familiar enough to the Egyptians, for whom Pharaoh was a god

30

Slaves building for the Egyptians: from a fresco in the tomb of Rekh-mi-Re at Thebes, 15th century BC.

incarnate, absolute ruler of his subjects, who through his hereditary bureaucracy directed the work of the illiterate masses to whatever projects were conceived to be in the national interest or favourable to his own prestige. But when the people of Israel looked back on their stay in Egypt from their settled position in their own country, they saw slavery as something alien and repulsive, and not so much a normal aspect of Egyptian society as a cruel measure directed against their ancestors out of special malice. An autocratic ruler who got the nation's work done by the slave labour of a subject people had no place in the concept of law and society which the Israelites had developed. We can feel the *frisson* of revulsion in the way the story of the enslavement is told – which was the way it was remembered and handed down.

The story of Pharaoh's ordering that every new-born Hebrew child should be cast into the river can be no part of the original story of the exodus and of Moses' part in it. Quite apart from the fact that it makes no sense to diminish the number of your slaves in this way – the more slaves breed, the better for the slave-owners – it is clearly a prelude to the hiding of the infant Moses in the ark of bulrushes, and that incident has so many counterparts in folklore throughout the world that it must be interpreted as an attempt to provide an impressive childhood for Moses, one that would explain why he, though a Hebrew, was master of all the arts of the Egyptians and had ready access to Pharaoh himself. He was hidden by the river to escape slaughter, in an ark of bulrushes daubed

Pharaoh's daughter finds Moses in the Nile: a fresco at Dura-Europos, Syria, 3rd century.

with slime and pitch, and was found there by Pharaoh's daughter when she came down to wash herself at the river. When she saw the baby, it wept; and she had compassion on it, though she knew it was a Hebrew baby; so she took it back to the palace and adopted it as her own child.

A similar story is told of King Sargon of Akkad (*c.* 2330 BC), known in two incomplete Neo-Assyrian copies and a Neo-Babylonian fragment (translated by E.M. Speiser):

> Sargon, the mighty king, king of Agade, am I.
> My mother was a changeling, my father I knew not.
> The brothers of my father loved the hills.
> My city is Azupiranu, which is situated on the banks of the Euphrates.
> My changeling mother conceived me, in secret she bore me.
> She set me in a basket of rushes, with bitumen she sealed my lid.
> She cast me into the river which rose not over me . . .

Sargon is rescued by Akki, the drawer of water, and brought up as his son.

There are many other such tales, both oriental and occidental, from the Indian epic *Mahabharata* (story of the son of the king's daughter Kunti) to the Greek myth of Dionysus, shut up in a chest with his mother and cast adrift on the waves, but rescued and nursed by her sister Ino. Theodore Gaster, in his study of myth, legend and custom in the Old Testament, has explained this

32

kind of story: 'In order, apparently, to enhance the wonder of the hero's
career, popular story loved to relate how he was exposed at birth and rescued
from imminent death only by what might seem to vulgar eyes an accident,
but what was really the hand of Fate interposed to preserve him for his high
destiny.' The use of such a story in telling of the infancy and childhood of
Moses is testimony to the strong sense of destiny colouring the Moses traditions and of the compulsion felt by the people who handed down those
traditions to illustrate their awareness of this destiny as vividly as possible.
The details are not historical; but they illustrate a popular feeling that attaches
itself to history and ultimately derives from historical events. It is significant,
too, that the mythical element, so common in other versions of this story, is
completely lacking: the story is told with quiet realism, and the irony of the
fact that it is the daughter of the despot himself who rescues the child and

Moses found in the bulrushes: from a 12th-century Byzantine bible.

brings him up in the despot's palace reflects the strength of the tradition that Moses the Hebrew was also in some sense an Egyptian, and that in this paradox lay his special powers.

We are told of Moses' genealogy at first in the simplest terms. 'And there went a man of the house of Levi, and took to wife a daughter of Levi. And the woman conceived and bare a son.' Levi was one of the sons of Jacob. All we are told here is that both Moses' parents were descended from him. Only in a later chapter are we given their names and some more details. What we have in this bare statement (Exodus 2: 1–2) is clearly an early tradition. We hear nothing at this stage of any brother or sister. Indeed, the way the story of Moses' birth is told here suggests very strongly that he is the eldest son. A man of the house of Levi married a wife of the house of Levi, 'and the woman conceived and bare a son'. Yet in 2: 4 we are told that when the child was set by the river 'his sister stood afar off, to know what would be done to him', and when the sister sees that Pharaoh's daughter is going to take the child she offers to get a Hebrew nurse for him, and gets the child's own mother. So the sister (not here named) is here conceived of as a fairly responsible young lady. We hear nothing at all of an older brother Aaron at this stage. The baby is brought home by Pharaoh's daughter, 'and he became her son. And she called his name Moses, and said, "Because I drew him out of the water."' The Hebrew word for 'I drew him out' is *meshitihu*, from *masha*, 'to draw out'. In fact, the Hebrew for Moses, *Moshe*, does not mean 'one who is drawn out', but 'one who draws out'. This is rather muddled folk etymology (and incidentally based on the assumption that the Egyptian princess spoke Hebrew). But in recording the fact that Moses was given his name by an Egyptian princess the biblical narrator is attesting a genuine tradition – that Moses is in fact an Egyptian name.

The name is probably the same as that found as the final element in such Egyptian names as *Ptah-mose* ('Ptah is born'); the Egyptians pronounced it *Mâse*, then, after the twelfth century BC, *Môse*: we can account for the shift from the *s* sound in the Egyptian to the *sh* sound in the Hebrew *Moshe* by the ambiguities involved in transcribing from Egyptian into Canaanite alphabetic characters. It has been argued that later Israelite tradition deliberately invented the Hebrew etymology of the name *Moshe*, the one who draws out, to indicate that he was the one who drew Israel forth from the flood (i.e. the Red Sea). However that may be, the tradition preserved in Chapter 2 of Exodus is unequivocally that Moses was a Hebrew brought up under strong Egyptian influence. And this is not an uncommon pattern among liberators

OPPOSITE Raphael's representation of the finding of Moses.

of oppressed peoples: they are often assimilated and privileged members of the oppressed people who are brought to realize their community with that people by some painful event and then use their knowledge of and influence among the ruling classes to effect liberation. (It may not be too far-fetched to place Theodore Herzl, the founder of modern Zionism and an assimilated Austrian Jew, in this category.)

It is at a considerably later stage in the story of Moses that we are given details about his parentage. Exodus 6 tells of Levi's three sons, Gershon, Kohath and Merari and of Kohath's four sons of whom the eldest was Amram. Amram married Jochebed, his father's sister. (Such a marriage is prohibited in Leviticus 18: 12, but as the Law had not yet been promulgated, presumably it was all right at this time; it has been argued that the very fact that such a marriage is against the Mosaic law is testimony to the truth of the biblical story, for nobody would want to invent such a discreditable feature of the hero's ancestry.) And Amram and Jochebed were Moses' father and mother. In this chapter too (verse 20) we hear of Aaron as Moses' elder brother. There is nothing here about a sister. Now it may be that this whole section is a later insertion emphasizing the Levitical genealogy of the hero, and certainly it is odd to find Moses represented as a great-grandson of Levi and thus only of the third generation after the original Israelite settlement in Egypt, whereas in Exodus 12: 40 we are told that the children of Israel sojourned in Egypt four hundred and thirty years. But that there are some genuine traditions preserved here is undeniable. First of all there are the Egyptian names associated with the family of Levi, such as Merari and Phinehas (verse 25). Phinehas (Hebrew *Pinechas*) is especially interesting: it is from Egyptian *Pi-nechase*, 'the Nubian', and provides independent confirmation of the tradition of a Nubian element in the family of Moses (we shall meet with this in a significant episode later). Interesting in a very different way is the name given to Moses' mother, Jochebed. If, as is very likely, the first element in this name derives from 'Yahweh', the name by which God revealed himself to Moses when he was staying with Jethro in Midian, it may well be that we are here dealing with a tradition that Moses' mother derived from the Midianites (or Kenites, as the Bible also calls them) and that they had previously worshipped God as Yahweh. If so, that would explain why Moses fled to Midian after he got into trouble in Egypt. He would have gone to his mother's people.

Moses fled to Midian after he had acted on his realization of the significance of his own Hebrew identity. Privileged and pampered as he was, something

OPPOSITE Luxor: the gateway to the temple of Ramesses II.

OVERLEAF *Israel in Egypt* by Sir Edward Poynter.

made him realize his relationship with the unfortunate Hebrew slaves. 'And it came to pass in those days when Moses was grown, that he went out unto his brethren, and looked on their burdens: and he spied an Egyptian smiting a Hebrew, one of his brethren. And he looked this way and that way, and when he saw that there was no man, he slew the Egyptian, and hid him in the sand.' (The verb is the same in Hebrew for the Egyptian smiting the Hebrew and Moses killing the Egyptian: it must mean 'kill' in both cases.)

And when he went out the second day, behold, two men of the Hebrews strove together: and he said to him that did the wrong, Wherefore smitest thou thy fellow? And he said, Who made thee a prince and a judge over us? intendest thou to kill me, as thou killedst the Egyptian? And Moses feared, and said, Surely this thing is known. Now when Pharaoh heard this thing, he sought to slay Moses. But Moses fled from the face of Pharaoh and dwelt in the land of Midian.

The concise biblical narrative is packed with meaning. Moses, excited by a presumably newly realized sense of identity with his fellow Hebrews, takes the side of an abused Hebrew slave and kills the slave-driver who is abusing him. The next day he learns that there is no necessary gratitude on the part of the oppressed towards the man who comes into conflict with authority on his behalf. This may well make the lot of the oppressed much worse. You do not liberate a people by an impulsive resort to individual violence. And people are not grateful for help which may appease your own sense of guilt but which does not improve their lot. There is considerable psychological perceptiveness in the account of the two episodes. We learn much about both Moses and the oppressed Hebrews. Moses has to undergo a quite different kind of education before he will be fit to liberate his people from slavery. And even then he will always be subject to intermittent protests from the liberated, for in some ways freedom is more difficult to bear than slavery. The theme of the 'murmurings' of the children of Israel against Moses is set thus early in the story, and in a context which introduces also another important theme in the biblical story, the education of Moses to be liberator and lawgiver. The other point about this episode is its total credibility, its lack of any mythological element, its presentation of Moses as impulsive and fallible and not someone who was heroically wise from the beginning.

The Midianites appear in the Bible as a nomadic people whom it is difficult to pin down to any one region because of the wide range of their wanderings. The 'land of Midian' to which Moses fled was probably in the south-eastern part of the Sinai Peninsula, although the main home of the Midianites is more

Moses and the burning bush: a 13th-century stained-glass window from Canterbury Cathedral.

41

The child Moses on the Nile, by Doré.

likely to have been on the eastern side of the Gulf of Aqaba. But the main point about Midian is that it represented for Moses a simple way of life and a stern desert moral code in sharpest contrast to the cosmopolitan syncretic polytheism of the Egypt he had grown up in, with its obsession with funerary rituals and the cult of the dead. The Midianite way of life as shepherds and smiths was much more like that of his Hebrew ancestors before they settled in Egypt. It is not improbable that Moses had learned something of his ancestral traditions from his mother (the tradition that, though brought up by Pharaoh's daughter, he was nursed by his real mother suggests this; and how else would he have known that he was a Hebrew though not a slave?). But whether Moses' experience in Midian represented in some way a picking up of the threads of an ancestral Hebrew cult, half forgotten during the long Hebrew residence in Egypt, or whether it represented a quite new kind of spiritual intuition, connected or unconnected with the simple Midianite culture, there can be little doubt that the tradition of Moses fleeing from Egypt to undergo some kind of inward transformation alone in the desert is absolutely central to the Moses story and must represent a basic truth.

The account of Moses' arrival in Midian is presented with a pastoral simplicity and directness reminiscent of similar stories told of the Patriarchs, notably that of Jacob at the well in Genesis 24. But there is a difference. In Jacob's case it is the girl, Rebekah, who befriends him and draws water for him. And Moses appears, not as the recipient of an almost symbolic favour, but as a deliverer in an unpleasantly real situation:

The finding of the infant Moses by the Pharaoh's daughter, by Bartholomew Breenbergh.

But Moses fled from the face of Pharaoh, and dwelt in the land of Midian: and he sat down by a well. Now the priest of Midian had seven daughters: and they came and drew water, and filled the troughs to water their father's flock. And the shepherds came and drove them away: but Moses stood up and helped them, and watered their flock. And when they came to Reuel their father, he said, How is it that ye are come so soon to-day? And they said, An Egyptian delivered us out of the hand of the shepherds, and also drew water enough for us, and watered the flock. And he said unto his daughters, And where is he? why is it that ye have left the man? call him, that he may eat bread. And Moses was content to dwell with the man: and he gave Moses Zipporah his daughter.

The seven girls were accustomed to be bullied by the shepherds and to have to wait until they had watered their flocks before they could proceed to water their own, so they returned unexpectedly early as a result of Moses' assistance. This is a nice touch, and shows a realistic rather than a mythological tradition at work. So is the girls' description of Moses as an Egyptian: he would have been dressed as one and spoken as one, having been brought up at Pharaoh's court and just arrived from Egypt. When Moses settled down with Reuel (or Jethro, as he is called in Exodus 3:1, or Hobab, as he is called in Judges 4:11: we shall call him henceforth Jethro, his more usual name) he was repudiating the Egyptian culture in the midst of which he had spent his childhood and youth in favour of a simple pastoral life. He became a shepherd.

The story carries its own conviction, but it is perhaps worth pointing to a

Moses at the well: detail from a fresco in the Sistine Chapel by Botticelli.

kind of parallel in the Egyptian story of Si-Nuhe, an Egyptian official of the Middle Kingdom (first part of the second millenium BC) who went into exile in Asia. In John A. Wilson's translation:

I set out at evening time, and when day broke I reached Peten. I halted at the Island of Kem-wer. An attack of thirst overtook me. I was parched, and my throat was dusty. . . . But then I lifted up my heart and collected myself, for I had heard the sound of the lowing of cattle, and I spied Asiatics. The sheikh among them, who had been in Egypt, recognized me. Then he gave me water while he boiled milk for me. I went with him to his tribe. What they did for me was good.

44

Si-Nuhe travels on further and comes to Qedem ('the East') where a local ruler befriends him:

He set me at the head of his children. He married me to his eldest daughter. He let me choose for myself of his country, of the choicest of that which was with him on his frontier with another country.

There is no parallel, however, to the biblical account of Moses' experience at the 'mountain of God'. But before we are told of this we are told, first of the birth of Moses' son Gershom ('for he said, I have been a stranger in a strange land': Hebrew *ger*, 'stranger', *sham*, 'there'), then, in what looks like an addition by the relatively late priestly writer generally known simply as 'P', whose constant aim is to emphasize the working out of a divine plan in all this history and whose chief interest is in the detailing of divine ordinances, we are reminded of what is going on in Egypt during Moses' long residence in Midian. It is a piece of 'continuity' writing, so that the reader cannot fail to see the divine pattern about to work itself out:

And it came to pass in process of time, that the king of Egypt died: and the children of Israel sighed by reason of the bondage, and they cried, and their cry came up unto God by reason of the bondage. And God heard their groaning, and God remembered his convenant with Abraham, with Isaac, and with Jacob. And God looked upon the children of Israel, and God had respect unto them [Exodus 2: 23–5].

A new note sounds in the account of Moses' experience at the mountain of God. Even the most rigorously scientific of modern biblical scholars recognize in this experience the genuinely ancient core of the Moses tradition and its starting point. The story had to get Moses to Midian, for it was there, alone in the wilderness, that his encounter with God took place. The biblical details of events which led up to Moses leaving Egypt for Midian we can accept in whatever degree we please; what they lead to is what matters.

Now Moses kept the flock of Jethro his father-in-law, the priest of Midian: and he led the flock to the back side of the desert, and came to the mountain of God, [even to Horeb]. And the Angel of the Lord appeared unto him in a flame of fire out of the midst of a bush: and he looked, and, behold, the bush burned with fire, and the bush was not consumed. And Moses said, I will now turn aside, and see this great sight, why the bush is not burnt. And when the Lord saw that he turned aside to see, God called him out of the midst of the bush, and said, Moses, Moses. And he said, Here am I. And he said, Draw not nigh hither: put off thy shoes from off thy feet; for the place whereon thou standest is holy ground. Moreover he said, I am the God of thy father, the God of Abraham, the God of

Isaac, and the God of Jacob. And Moses hid his face, for he was afraid to look upon God.

We do not know where this mountain of God was. It is highly probable that the phrase 'even to Horeb' (put in square brackets in the quotation above) is a later, and rather lame, addition, by a redactor who wished to emphasize the identity of this mountain with Mount Sinai, where Moses was later to lead his people and where the Law was delivered: the names Sinai and Horeb are used interchangeably in the Bible. We do not know where Sinai is either, for that matter; as we shall see, there are many different theories as to which mountain is meant. But this is not important. Moses, the shepherd, accidentally leads his flock to a mountain which has special divine associations. There is a rabbinical tradition that while looking after the flock Moses discovered that a young lamb had escaped; he followed it, and found it quenching its thirst at a stream. 'If I had known that you were thirsty,' he said to the lamb, 'I would have taken you in my arms and carried you here.' On which a heavenly voice called out: 'As thou livest, thou art fit to be shepherd to Israel.' This emphasizes the strong biblical association between shepherd and leader-cum-protector ('The Lord is my shepherd'). Moses' skill, conscientiousness and compassion as a shepherd help to qualify him for the task he is now to be called upon to perform.

It is '*the* mountain of God', not '*a* mountain of God', just as in the original Hebrew (though not in the English translation) the burning bush is from the beginning referred to as '*the* bush'. Moreover, the word used for the bush, *seneh*, means a particular kind of bush. It has been variously identified as the wild jujube (*Zizyphus spina-Christi*) known in both Arabic and Egyptian as *nabs* ('the god Safdu who dwells in the *nabs*,' reads an ancient inscription found in the Sinai desert, and in Deuteronomy 33: 16 God is described as 'he that dwelt in the *seneh*'); a variety of acacia, the climber *Loranthus acaciae*, which is covered with red flowers and fruit so that from a distance it can look as though it is burning; the low desert plant *cassia obocata*; the yellow-flowered shrub *colutea istria*; or the simple bramble, which is the oldest known traditional Jewish view. It is possible that the early writers saw a connection between the word *seneh* and the word Sinai. But what is most important is the nature of the experience involved. The angel (or messenger) of God takes the form of a perpetually burning fire in the bush; Moses' curiosity is aroused by seeing the bush burn without being consumed, so he turns aside to go and look more closely. And then God calls to him. God does not appear as a physical form. (True, Moses hides his face for he is afraid to look upon God, but there is no suggestion that a physically visible God is there to be looked on.)

Moses and the burning bush: engraved after a painting by John Martin.

God tells Moses that he has seen the affliction of his people in Egypt; he has heard their cry; he knows their sorrows. And he is now going to deliver them from Egypt 'unto a good land and a large'. He proposes to send Moses to Pharaoh, to bring the people out of Egypt. Moses protests. 'Who am I, that I should go unto Pharaoh, and that I should bring forth the children of Israel out of Egypt?' God replies that he will be with him, and guarantees that after Moses has brought the people out of Egypt they shall worship God on this very mountain. Moses, still reluctant, protests a second time. 'Behold, when I

47

come unto the children of Israel, and shall say unto them, The God of your fathers has sent me unto you; and they shall say to me, What is his name? what shall I say unto them. And God said unto Moses, I AM THAT I AM: and he said, Thus shalt thou say unto the children of Israel, I AM hath sent me unto you.'

Moses continues to resist, but before we follow this aspect of the story we must pause to consider this question of God's name, for the originality of Moses' interpretation of the divine is bound up with the name used for God.

In the traditional English versions of the Bible, the word 'God' translates the Hebrew word *elohim*, which is the plural of a lengthened form of *el* (strong one, mighty one, hero, god) but is used in the Bible as a singular to mean 'the Divinity' or 'the Godhead'. The Hebrew word translated as 'Lord' in the Bible is the name which God specifically revealed to Moses (Exodus 3:15 and 6:3) as the name by which he had not been known to the Patriarchs. This name can be transliterated in English as YHWH or JHVH, since Hebrew was written in consonants only. These four letters, known as the 'Tetragrammaton', we know from Greek transliterations to have been pronounced something like 'Yahweh'. But at a fairly early stage it came to be regarded as improper for God's mystical name Yahweh to be pronounced, and instead one had to say the word *Adonai* ('my lord(s)'). Now, when the Hebrew text of the Bible came to have vowel points inserted, to facilitate reading of its hitherto purely consonantal text, the vowels of the word *Adonai* were inserted underneath the consonants YHWH or JHVH as an indication that the reader must say *Adonai* and not *Yahweh*. Christian translators of the Bible, not understanding that the vowels put under the consonants YHWH or JHVH did not belong to those consonants but were the vowels of *Adonai*, put together the vowels of *Adonai* and the consonants JHVH to make a non-existent word *Jehovah*, which is in fact an impossible Hebrew form.

It is interesting that God tells Moses 'I am that I am' and orders him to tell the children of Israel that '"I am" hath sent me to you' *before* he reveals to him his name of Yahweh. But the phrase translated 'I am that I am', in Hebrew *Ehyeh asher ehyeh*, is clearly meant to be a clue to the meaning of God's name *Yahweh* and may perhaps help us to understand its etymology. Albright has pointed out that if the phrase is transposed into the old Hebrew causative mood it becomes *Yahweh asher yihweh* (later *yihyeh*), 'He Causes to be what Comes into Existence'. When the old Hebrew causative ceased to be used, the phrase was modified to the form in which it appears in Exodus 3:14. If this is indeed the true history of the sentence traditionally rendered as 'I am that I am', then God in making this statement to Moses is preparing him for his

Raphael's painting of the burning bush episode, in the Vatican.

subsequent revelation of his name Yahweh and at the same time emphasizing his role as the sole creator of all. But he is also emphasizing his special relationship with Israel and his identity with the God discovered by the Patriarchs. The God of the fathers, God the creator of all, and God the protector of Israel are revealed as one and the same. Was this an original contribution by Moses to the development of the religion of Israel?

When God emphasizes his name Yahweh to Moses in Chapter 6 of Exodus he says: 'I am Yahweh: And I appeared unto Abraham, unto Isaac, and unto Jacob, by the name of El Shaddai [translated in the Authorized Version as' 'God Almighty']; but by my name Yahweh I was not known to them.' Now in fact the name Yahweh is used in Genesis with reference to the Patriarchs, who are shown as having known and employed it as well as other divine names such as El Shaddai (which is now thought to have meant originally 'God of the Mountain') and El Elyon ('the Highest God'). Conservative theologians who are reluctant to accept the view held by most scholars that there are clear traces of different hands at work in the redaction of the traditions of the people of Israel in Genesis, Exodus and subsequent books of the Bible, explain the apparent contradiction of God's telling Moses that he was not known as Yahweh to Abraham, Isaac and Jacob although Genesis tells us clearly that he *was* so known to the Patriarchs by arguing that what God said to Moses meant that he had not been fully known and understood before as Yahweh, the true significance of the name (which has implications of perpetual existence and continual presence as well as causing to be) not being appreciated by them, even though they used it. Martin Buber argues more sophisticatedly that while the name Yahweh had been known to the Hebrews earlier, during their long stay in Egypt 'it had become empty and half forgotten. Under such conditions an hour might well come when the people would ask this question of a man bringing them a message from the God of their fathers: "How about his name?" That means: "What is this God really like? We cannot find out from his name!" For as far as primitive human beings are concerned, the name of a person indicates his character.' So we can explain the presence of the name Yahweh in Genesis either by saying that the writer who wrote those parts of Genesis in which it appears was a 'Yahwist' (known as 'J') retroactively applying the name that emerged at the time of Moses, or by arguing that in some way Moses resuscitated and reinterpreted a traditional Hebrew divine name that had been used before but not with this new implication. The two views are not, of course, mutually incompatible. What is indisputable is the tradition that Moses brought to his people ideas about God's name and nature (and name and nature were in those days inextricably intertwined) that they had not known before. The distinguished historian of Israel John Bright has well summed the matter up: 'We really do not know whether a God called Yahweh had been worshipped before Moses or not. But, if such was the case, we may be certain that through the work of Moses, Yahwism was completely transformed and given a new content. It is with Moses that Israel's distinctive faith begins.'

It is tempting to associate Moses' new conception of God with his stay among the Midianites. His father-in-law Jethro is said to have been a priest of Midian (Exodus 2: 16), though we are not informed of the name and nature of the God he served. There is evidence that Sinai and Midian were at this time inhabited by semi-sedentary tribes who, though their lives and culture were very much simpler than the complexly sophisticated civilization of Egypt, were far from barbaric. Archaeological evidence confirms the working of copper mines east of the Gulf of Aqaba. The Bible repeatedly calls the Midianites 'Kenites', which apparently means 'belonging to the copper-smiths'. Moses' marriage to a daughter of a priest of Midian, whether called Jethro or Reuel or Hobab (this last probably, however, being the *son* of Jethro-Reuel), is well attested. Indeed, there are three different biblical testimonies to the fact that Moses took a foreign wife. The first is the one we have already quoted: she is a Midianite. The second, found in Numbers 12, is that she was an Ethiopian or Cushite. The third, found in Judges 1: 16 and 4: 11, is that she was a Kenite. Now, as Martin Noth has pointed out, it is highly unlikely that Moses had *three* foreign wives. 'Rather, we have here in three different narrative versions the same original element of tradition concerning Moses' foreign marriage relationship, which, being triply attested, is made all the more reliable.' So Moses lived for many years in the most intimate association with a people who led simple but far from uncivilized lives, and his wife was a daughter of a priest of that people. If, as we have already suggested, Moses fled from Egypt to Midian because he had ancestral connections there through his mother, whose name appears to indicate a belief in Yahweh, he may have rediscovered there some earlier traditions of the Habiru and given them new definition and meaning. This so-called 'Kenite hypothesis' is purely a matter of conjecture, and it can never be conclusively either proved or disproved.

We return to the reluctant Moses at the burning bush. After God has declared 'I am that I am' he goes on to amplify his charge to Moses:

Thus shalt thou say unto the children of Israel, Yahweh God of your fathers, the God of Abraham, the God of Isaac, and the God of Jacob, hath sent me unto you: this is my name for ever, and this is my memorial unto all generations. Go, and gather the elders of Israel together, and say unto them, Yahweh God of your fathers, the God of Abraham, of Isaac, and of Jacob, appeared unto me saying,

I have surely visited you, and seen that which is done to you in Egypt. And I have said, I will bring you up out of the affliction of Egypt into the land of the Canaanites, and the Hittites, and the Amorites, and the Perrizzites, and the Hivites, and the Jebusites, unto a land flowing with milk and honey. [We need not worry at this stage about identifying these peoples; the list of them early became a formula, added more or less automatically to every reference to the Promised Land.] And they shall hearken to thy voice: and thou shalt come, thou and the elders of Israel, unto the king of Egypt, and ye shall say unto him, Yahweh God of the Hebrews hath met with us: and now let us go, we beseech thee, three days' journey into the wilderness, that we may sacrifice to Yahweh our God.

God goes on to predict that Pharaoh will not let them go, but that he (God) will stretch out his hand and smite Egypt with all his wonders 'and after that he will let you go'.

Moses replies that the people will not listen to him. God then provides Moses with three signs of authentication: his rod – his shepherd's crook – turns into a snake and back into a rod; his hand becomes leprous and is then made whole again; and he is told that if these two signs fail he will be able to turn water into blood as further proof of his divine mission. Here we seem to be dealing in pure folklore. As Theodore Gaster has put it:

It is a common feature of folktales all over the world that a hero has to qualify for his mission by performing a set of seemingly impossible *tasks*. . . . It may therefore be suggested that it was a threefold test of this kind that popular fancy originally associated with the selection and appointment of the Israelite leader. Subsequently, however, the real point of the story came to be forgotten, and the miraculous feats performed by Moses were represented as tokens of authentication graciously vouchsafed to him by Yahweh.

The real point of the three signs, however, is to emphasize Moses' obstinacy in his modesty. He is neither conceited nor ambitious; tradition from a very early stage emphasized his *meekness*; and he actually provokes God to anger by his persistent reluctance to accept his commission as a leader. He protests now that he is 'slow of speech, and of a slow tongue'. God counters by saying, 'Who hath made man's mouth? or who maketh the dumb, or deaf, or the seeing, or the blind? have not I Yahweh? Now therefore go, and I will be with thy mouth, and teach thee what thou shalt say.' Moses replies ambiguously by saying, 'O my Lord [not 'Yahweh' this time, but the normal form of respectful address to a

superior], send, I pray thee, by the hand of him whom thou wilt send.'
He is saying, rather deviously, 'Send anyone but me.' 'And the anger of
the Lord was kindled against Moses, and he said, Is there not Aaron thy
brother the Levite?' Aaron, God goes on to say, will do the actual speaking for Moses: God will put the words into Moses' mouth, and Moses
will then tell Aaron.

This is an odd conclusion to a classic example of a hero's modest reluctance.
It looks very much as though Aaron – not mentioned earlier – is introduced
here by a later hand in order that he may have a part in the story from the
beginning. Indeed, it seems probable that both Miriam and Aaron were at
first quite independent figures. (Miriam is 'Miriam the prophetess' in Exodus
15: 20 when she goes out with timbrels and dances to celebrate deliverance
from the Egyptians in the crossing of the sea, and this, as we shall see, is one of
the oldest passages in the Bible.) They were probably added to Moses' family
later, and may well have played parts in their own right in earlier accounts
which have not survived. Aaron's function in the confrontation with Pharaoh
certainly seems confused. The whole thing looks like an attempt by the
priestly writer P to claim some of the credit for the deliverance from Egypt
for the traditional founder of the priesthood, Aaron. Aaron's presence takes
just a little of the limelight away from Moses, though Moses remains the hero
of the exodus.

3

'Let my people go'

About four centuries elapsed before the orally transmitted accounts of Moses' life were put into writing; these accounts themselves came down in three traditions, and though there are some contradictions and confusions among them, these are less important than the strength of their combined testimony. That Moses led his people out of Egypt and in doing so gave them a new religious consciousness is a belief that stands at the core of Israel's historical memory. The association of the exodus from Egypt with both divine revelation and the birth of a nation can be traced back from known history to inferred history. 'A belief so ancient and so entrenched,' John Bright has remarked, 'will admit of no explanation save that Israel actually escaped from Egypt to the accompaniment of events so stupendous that they were impressed forever on her memory.'

An interesting example of the uncertainty of the tradition about minor details (which brings into greater relief its certainty about the central events) is the apparent contradiction in the information provided about the whereabouts of Moses' family after his decision to leave Midian and return to Egypt to liberate his people. According to Exodus 4: 20 'Moses took his wife and his sons, and set them upon an ass, and he returned to the land of Egypt.' According to Exodus 18: 2 Moses sent his wife Zipporah back to stay with his father-in-law Jethro. An ancient and puzzling tale has found its way into the biblical account of Moses returning to Egypt with his wife and child, and anthropologists have had a field-day with it. Here is the account in Exodus 4: 21–6 in the language of the Authorized Version:

And the Lord said unto Moses, When thou goest to return unto Egypt, see that thou do all those wonders before Pharaoh, which I have put in thine hand: but I will harden his heart, that he shall not let the people go. And thou shalt say unto Pharaoh, Thus saith the Lord, Israel is my son, even my firstborn. And it came to pass, by the way in the inn, that the Lord met him, and sought to kill him. Then Zipporah took a sharp stone and cut off the foreskin of her son, and cast it at his feet, and said, Surely a bloody husband art thou to me. So he let him go: then she said, A bloody husband thou art, because of the circumcision.

This is not the place to go into the complex question of ritual circumcision in the ancient world: Israel was only one among very many nations who practised it, and from an early period it was regarded in Israelite tradition as the sign of a covenant between God on the one hand and Abraham and his descendants on the other (see Genesis 18: 11–12). But it is worth noting that the biblical prescription of circumcision is at odds with the whole tenor of biblical repudiation of ritual practices common among the pagan neighbours of the Israelites and the fierce prohibition of any kind of bodily mutilation, whether ritual or not (even tattooing and scarification were forbidden on these grounds). The prohibition even extended to animals. The origins of the practice of circumcision, and its adoption in Israelite tradition, remain mysterious. The story of Moses and Zipporah and her son told in Exodus 4 is doubly mysterious, for it puts the puzzling practice into an even more puzzling context. We can clarify it in some degree by correcting a misunderstanding of earlier translators. The phrase rendered 'a bloody husband art thou to me' represents a misunderstanding of the word *chatan*, which, it is true, in Hebrew means 'bridegroom' or 'husband' but which here is clearly cognate with the Arabic *chatana*, 'circumcise'. Zipporah was a Midianite (her Hebrew name, Zipporah, 'little bird', is a kind of generalized Hebrew name of affection which probably developed later in the tradition) and for her the word *chatan* would have meant 'circumcision'. The sentence she uttered, then, meant something like, 'You are mine, circumcised with blood'. The next stresses that it is Zipporah who keeps talking about *chatan* and she goes on to explain that this is *her* word for 'circumcision' ('a *chatan* of blood, because of the circumcision'). Why should she have said that? In the verse immediately preceding the account of the Lord's seeking to kill Moses and being prevented by the circumcision, we hear of God's threat to slay Pharaoh's firstborn son. If we take the 'him' in 'sought to kill him' to be Moses' son and not Moses himself – and this makes most sense – it looks as though we are dealing here with a ritual attempt to prevent the son of Moses and his wife (who was a Midianite, and therefore not entitled to the special treatment and exceptions reserved for the Hebrews during the plagues) from being killed as the Egyptian firstborn were later killed. If this is so, it is chronologically out of order, but its presence among the Moses traditions can be explained. Moses' son is saved from the fate of the Egyptians by being certified a Hebrew through ritual circumcision.

Other explanations of this mysterious passage have been offered, but we must not allow them to detain us, because the passage itself is not central to the story of Moses and his achievement as it was handed down. But it is worth pausing a moment to note that if we take the 'him' of the 'sought to kill him' to mean Moses, then it is Yahweh himself who is said to have sought Moses' life – the life of the very man whom he has recently commissioned to liberate his people. Martin Buber accepts this, and argues that the story is basically one of nocturnal struggle on the part of a man of God with his own doubts, comparable to that which Jacob endured when he wrestled with the mysterious stranger (Genesis 32: 24). Buber points out that early Israelite religion knew no Satan, and that Yahweh represented *all* power, both beneficent and threatening, and that some of those powers it is proper to withstand, and he cites in this connection the strange words put into God's mouth in Isaiah 45: 5: 'I form the light, and create darkness; I make peace, and create evil. I Yahweh do all these things.'

Ideas of this kind, however obscure, remind us when we encounter them in the biblical story of Moses of the oddity and originality of the concept of the divine mediated by Moses. It is tempting to suggest that Moses must have picked up his ideas from those current in the Egyptian circles in which he was brought up, and that his concept of a single all-powerful Yahweh derives from Akhenaten's view of Aten as the all-powerful 'Master of Heaven, Master of the Earth' (*Hymn to the Aten*, translated by W.K.Simpson). But in spite of some similarities of phrasing between some descriptions of Aten and some descriptions of God in the Psalms, the differences are fundamental. The story of Yahweh's relations with Moses and with his people and of the covenant he makes with them as told in Exodus is like no other myth or legend or story or tradition in the history of any other of the Middle Eastern peoples. For all the parallels and similarities that we naturally find between Israel's beliefs and that of her neighbours, Israel, in Martin Noth's words, remained 'a stranger in the world of its age, a stranger wearing the garments and behaving in the manner of its age, yet separate from the world it lived in'. We need not necessarily accept that the name Yahweh was first introduced by

Moses; but whether it was or not, he certainly both identified Yahweh with the ancestral 'God of the fathers' and gave his worship a new meaning. There seems to have been both a rediscovery and a reinterpretation of relations with the divine. This was a sort of 'syncretism', a bringing together of different elements from different traditions, but the significant thing is that it was a highly directed and limited syncretism. In H.H.Rowley's words: 'Yahweh never gathered Baal into Himself, and refused to be swallowed up by Baal. . . . All other gods, worshipped by other people, were entirely negligible. The gods of Egypt figure in the story of the deliverance of Israel, but Yahweh's conflict was not with them, but with Pharaoh, and they could be dropped from the story without varying its course.' Was the view of Yahweh presented by Moses then monotheism? The question presupposes a kind of theological sophistication that the early Israelites did not possess. Modern scholars distinguish between henotheism ('the exclusive worship of a tribal-national deity which did not deny the reality of patron deities of other people', in Bright's definition), 'monolatry' (belief in one god without necessarily denying the existence of others) and monotheism, belief that only one all-powerful God exists. But what was most important for the Mosaic tradition was the absoluteness of Yahweh's power, the absolute nature of his ethical demands and the special relationship he established with Israel. It was to demonstrate the first of these in particular that Yahweh allowed Pharaoh to continue to behave with cruel stubbornness towards the Hebrew slaves (symbolized by his hardening of Pharaoh's heart) until successive manifestations of divine power had come to a climax.

The biblical story of Moses' (and sometimes Aaron's) encounters with Pharaoh and of the ten plagues, which punish Pharaoh's refusal to accede to Yahweh's demands for the release of his people until finally Pharaoh in agony actually *drives* them out, cannot be in any literal sense historical. But history lies behind the story somewhere. Here we have a Hebrew, brought up as an Egyptian, discovering his community with his enslaved fellow Hebrews and as a result acting in such a way as to incur the wrath of authority. He flees to another country (where his mother's people came from?) and there, alone in the desert, has a mystical experience which convinces him, albeit reluctantly, that it is his duty to return to Egypt and liberate his fellow Hebrews. These themes are strongly developed and convincingly presented. The picture after this is somewhat less clear. Moses and Aaron gather the people together and convince them by the agreed 'signs' that they have a mission from Yahweh. 'And afterward, Moses and Aaron went in and told Pharaoh, Thus saith Yahweh, God of Israel, Let my people go, that they may hold a feast unto me in the wilderness.' This is apparently only a request for a short holiday in order

to observe a religious festival, and suggests either that Moses and Aaron are being devious or that a quite different tradition has crept in here. 'And Pharaoh said, Who is Yahweh, that I should obey his voice to let Israel go?' A good question: Yahweh was not the name of a god that could have been familiar to Pharaoh, for all the syncretism of Egyptian religion. 'And they said, The God of the Hebrews hath met with us: let us go, we pray thee, three days' journey into the desert, and sacrifice unto Yahweh our God; lest he fall upon us with pestilence, or with the sword.' There is nothing here about leaving the country permanently. Further the first person plural in 'met with us' and 'let us go' might suggest that here we have a tradition about negotiations with Pharaoh having started with a whole body of Israelites present. Moses is not mentioned in Exodus 5: 5–19, where we are told of Pharaoh's angry response to the request and his commanding the taskmasters to make the Hebrews henceforth gather their own straw for the bricks they had to make without diminishing the number of bricks completed, and in verses 19–20 we get an odd picture of 'the officers of the children of Israel' meeting Moses and Aaron, 'who stood in the way, as they came forth from Pharaoh', so that Moses is actually standing outside while representatives of the Hebrews negotiate with Pharaoh in the palace. Does this derive from a tradition of a pre-Mosaic attempt on the part of the Hebrews to negotiate not complete liberation but a few days' holiday for religious purposes? It is impossible to say. But it is interesting that in Exodus 6: 1 Yahweh tells Moses that he (Moses) will see what he is going to do to Pharaoh 'for with a strong hand shall he let them go, and with a strong hand shall he drive them out of his land', and immediately afterwards (6: 2–8) we have a repeat, as it were, of Yahweh's call to Moses already described in 3: 1 to 4: 16, but this time it is apparently set in Egypt. Another difference is that this time God specifically states that he was not known to the Patriarchs by his name Yahweh. We are clearly dealing here with a conflation of different traditions. Yet another tradition appears in Exodus 6: 14–25, with its lists of heads of houses and its mentioning for the first time of the names of Moses' parents in a context which shows Moses as only in the fourth generation from Jacob. In Exodus 7: 7 it is revealed for the first time that Aaron is the older brother. At the time of his call, Moses was eighty and Aaron eighty-three. We cannot, of course, take biblical ages literally, but the implication is interesting and represents what may well be an authentic tradition: that Moses had spent most of his adult life in Midian and was no longer a young man when he returned to Egypt.

The somewhat childish competition in conjuring tricks between Moses and

Moses and Aaron before Pharaoh, Aaron's rod transformed into a serpent, by Doré.

Aaron on the one hand and Pharaoh's magicians on the other is simple folk stuff, but it is the prelude to the account of the ten plagues that is pregnant with the conviction of divine power working for the Hebrews and against Pharaoh. The object of the plagues is expressed in Exodus 7: 5 with forceful directness: 'And the Egyptians shall know that I am Yahweh, when I stretch forth mine hand upon Egypt, and bring out the children of Israel from among them.' The plagues are not magic, nor on the other hand are they simply natural events, though they are based on natural events and represent a heightening and ordering and a deliberate turning on and turning off of events that could and did occur. They represent Yahweh at work on nature in order to manifest his total control of it. The plagues themselves are based on what was known of natural phenomena in Egypt – swarms of frogs, stinging flies, cattle pestilence, skin disease, locusts, a fatal children's epidemic. But it would be vain to try and account for the plagues wholly naturalistically. The tradition of the plagues is one of the divine manipulation of nature in order to prove something to Pharaoh and liberate the Israelites. It represents a conviction that entered deep into the historical consciousness of the people of Israel that the exodus from Egypt, as achieved by Moses, was something *special*, and was achieved as a result of special divine intervention.

The account of the plagues seems to have come down in a number of separate traditions. The account in Exodus gives ten plagues, beginning with the changing of all the waters of Egypt into blood and culminating in the death of the Egyptian firstborn. (There appear to be some inconsistencies even within the Exodus account, for we are told in 8: 19 that the act of turning water into blood was performed 'upon the waters of Egypt, upon their streams, upon their rivers, and upon their ponds, and upon all their pools of water', while in 7: 24 it is assumed that only the river water was turned to blood 'and all the Egyptians digged round about the river for water to drink'.) The second plague in the Exodus account is frogs, well known in Egypt as proliferating in the humidity resulting from the annual overflowing of the Nile and consequently of some significance in Egyptian mythology, but a much less significant phenomenon in Palestine. The third plague is lice. Then come what the Authorized Version calls 'swarms of flies' (the Hebrew word *'arov* is apparently connected with the root meaning 'to mix', and may therefore mean a mixture of noxious insects or other creatures), followed by a pestilence that killed the livestock, boils that afflicted both men and animals, hail and fire that smote man and beast as well as 'every herb of the field, and . . . every tree of the field'. A grievous plague of locusts followed, that consumed every green thing; then darkness, isolating every man from his neighbour; and finally the terrible slaying. A somewhat different version is found in Psalms 78: 44–51, which gives the order: blood, swarms of flies and frogs, caterpillars and locusts, hail and frost (?) and 'hot thunderbolts' (but the word so translated probably means 'pestilence'), death and pestilence, and the slaying of the firstborn. Here there is no clear division into ten, and sometimes more than one plague appears simultaneously. A third tradition, preserved in Psalms 106: 28–36, gives: darkness, blood, frogs, 'divers sorts of flies and lice', hail and fire, locusts and caterpillars, and the slaying of the firstborn, making seven plagues or groups of plagues.

The plague of frogs: an 18th-century engraving.

The plague of locusts: a 17th-century wood engraving (ABOVE); an illumination from the Nuremberg Bible, 1483 (BELOW).

The account in Exodus appears to be a composite account, compiled from three traditions, and is therefore the fullest; it is bound up at each stage with the confrontation between Moses and Pharaoh. In the first three plagues there is competition between Aaron, acting as Moses' second as it were, and Pharaoh's magicians who similarly act for him. Yahweh tells Moses to tell Aaron to stretch his rod over the waters of Egypt so that they will turn to blood. But then the magicians were able to do this too. After seven days, Yahweh told Moses to ask Pharaoh in the name of Yahweh to let his people go 'that they may serve me' and threatened the plague of frogs if the request was refused. There is no record of Pharaoh's reply, which must have been negative, for the plague of frogs duly followed. But the Egyptian magicians were also able to conjure forth frogs. Still they must have been unable to get rid of the masses of frogs that Aaron had brought up, for Pharaoh 'called for Moses and Aaron, and said, Entreat Yahweh, that he may take away the frogs from me, and from my people; and I will let the people go, that they may do sacrifice unto Yahweh'. Moses, to show Yahweh's power, asked Pharaoh for a definite time when the frogs should be destroyed or removed, and Pharaoh fixed the following day, to which Moses agreed. Moses appealed to Yahweh, and 'the frogs died out of the houses, out of the villages, and out of the fields'. A realistic detail suggests that some memory of a real plague of frogs lay behind the tradition: 'And they gathered them together upon heaps; and the land stank.'

Once he was rid of the frogs, Pharaoh hardened his heart and went back on his promise. So the third plague of lice followed. This time Pharaoh's magicians were unable to compete. 'And the magicians did so with their enchantments to bring forth lice, but they could not.' And the magicians admitted, 'This is the finger of God.' (Not, interestingly enough, 'the finger of Yahweh', but 'the finger of Elohim', a term for God that is more general and may be presumed to make no necessary admission of Yahweh's all-powerful status.) At this point the magicians retire from the proceedings, and so does Aaron: the conflict is now presented as between the two principals, Moses and Pharaoh. (When, in the sixth plague, Aaron re-enters the proceedings in a minor role, so do the magicians, but not for long.) The first three rounds – and the plagues are presented in Exodus as in three groups of three with a final terrible culminating one that is in a quite different category – end with victory for Moses. But Pharaoh is all the more angry and obstinate as a result: 'He hardened his heart at this time also, neither would he let the people go.'

The fourth plague, like the first, is preceded by God's command to Moses to go out in the morning to confront Pharaoh on his way to the river. He is to deliver the usual warning in the name of Yahweh. 'Let my people go, that they may serve me. Else, if thou wilt not let my people go, I will send swarms of flies upon thee, and upon thy servants, and upon thy people, and into thy houses. . . .' This time it is specifically mentioned that the land of Goshen, where the Israelites dwell, will be free of the flies, 'to the end that thou mayest know that I am Yahweh in the midst of the earth'. (A more adequate translation would be: 'that thou mayest know that I, Yahweh, am in the midst of the land'. The purpose of the separation of Goshen from the rest of Egypt is to demonstrate that Yahweh is there and is looking after his people.) Pharaoh summons Moses and Aaron and tells them they can go and sacrifice to their God – but 'in the land', not in the wilderness as Moses had demanded. Moses replies that it would be offensive to the Egyptians for them to sacrifice in Egypt: presumably they were to sacrifice a cow, which would give great offence to the Egyptians who regarded the animal as sacred to the god Isis. He insists that they go three days' journey into the wilderness in order to sacrifice to Yahweh, and Pharaoh, tormented by the swarms of flies (or whatever they are), concedes in a very human speech: 'I will let you go, that ye may sacrifice to Yahweh your God in the wilderness; only ye shall not go very far away: entreat for me.' Moses replies that he will indeed entreat Yahweh to remove the plague the next day, 'but let not Pharaoh deal deceitfully any more in not letting the people go to sacrifice to Yahweh'. But once the swarms were gone, 'Pharaoh hardened his heart at this time also, neither would he let the people go'.

The next plague, the murrain or pestilence on the cattle, follows a further warning to Pharaoh by Moses, which is ignored. Here again it is specifically mentioned that the cattle of the children of Israel were unharmed. 'And Pharaoh sent, and, behold, there was not one of the cattle of the Israelites dead. And the heart of Pharaoh was hardened, and he did not let the people go.' The narrator here introduces an interesting psychological touch: Pharaoh is so enraged at the sight of the Israelites' cattle being unscathed while the Egyptian cattle are smitten by pestilence that in spite of the plague he remains obstinate. (He is shown as having reacted similarly when he found that his magicians could not compete with Moses in bringing about the plague of lice.) So the next plague of boils follows (Egypt was known for its skin diseases: cf. Deuteronomy 28: 27). 'And Yahweh hardened the heart of Pharaoh' so that he still refused to let the people go.

The notion of God's deliberately hardening Pharaoh's heart and then punishing him for his consequent behaviour, which runs through the latter part of the story of the plagues, may strike the modern reader as implying a

OPPOSITE The burning bush, by Eustechio.

OVERLEAF The burning bush, another interpretation by Raphael.

very odd concept of justice. But it represents the biblical narrator's attempt to show that human events occur in conformity to God's design for history and at the same time that the individual is responsible for his actions. Not that any philosophical theories concerning the relationship between determinism and free will had been worked out at this time; there was just a general belief that God organized history and at the same time man was a responsible agent. The plagues unfolded as a punishment for Pharaoh's original cruel stubbornness and as a demonstration of Yahweh's power. One may also see in this concept of God's hardening Pharaoh's heart the same refusal to see a diabolical force of evil working against the divine intention, the same insistence that *everything* comes from God, which, as we noted earlier in this chapter, Martin Buber saw as the explanation of the mysterious events of Exodus 4: 21–6.

The seventh plague, the hail and fire, is preceded by a warning to Pharaoh by Yahweh through Moses longer and sterner than any yet given. And again the land of Goshen is spared. Under this grievous affliction (there had been nothing like it 'in all the land of Egypt since it became a nation') Pharaoh gives in, and makes a significant confession: 'I have sinned this time. Yahweh is righteous, and I and my people are wicked.' Moses agrees to entreat Yahweh to remove the plague, but adds grimly: 'But as for thee and thy servants, I know that ye will not yet fear Yahweh.' Yahweh has not yet finished with Pharaoh. He tells Moses: 'Go in unto Pharaoh: for I have hardened his heart, and the heart of his servants, that I might show these my signs before him: And that thou mayest tell in the ear of thy son, and of thy son's son, what things I have wrought in Egypt, and my signs which I have wrought among them; that ye may know that I am Yahweh.' Here surely we get something like the sound of the actual oral tradition as it was recited and handed down, with the naming of this central event in Israel's history as essentially something to be remembered and transmitted down the generations combined with a profession of faith in Yahweh's omnipotence.

The confrontation is now wrought up to a highly dramatic pitch. Moses (in 10: 3 it says Aaron as well, but it is clear from 10: 6 that only Moses is involved here and that it is a very personal matter between him and Pharaoh) transmits his message:

Thus says Yahweh God of the Hebrews, How long wilt thou refuse to humble thyself before me? let my people go, that they may serve me. Else, if thou refuse to let my people go, behold, tomorrow will I bring the locusts unto the coast: And they shall cover the face of the earth, that one cannot be able to see the earth: and they shall eat the residue of that which is escaped, which remaineth unto you from

OPPOSITE Mount Sinai, by El Greco.

The murrain of beasts, by Doré.

the hail, and shall eat every tree that groweth for you out of the field: And they shall fill thy houses, and the houses of all the Egyptians; which neither thy fathers, nor thy fathers' fathers have seen, since the day that they were upon the earth until this day. And he turned himself, and went out from Pharaoh.

Is this the imagination of a lively dramatic writer or do we hear in this passage a distant echo of a genuine confrontation, with Moses, threatening and indignant, delivering his warning with a bitter relish of its details before striding out, oblivious of protocol, from the king's presence?

However this may be, the narrator clearly enjoys the situation. Following the abrupt departure of Moses after his latest threat, the palace servants express to Pharaoh their unease about this sinister Hebrew stalking about the palace making dire prophecies which all come true. Let the Hebrew men go, anyway, they urge. So Pharaoh recalls Moses and says, 'Go, serve Yahweh your God: but who are they that shall go?' Moses replies that all the people will go,

The plague of hail and fire, by John Martin.

young and old, with their sons and daughters and their flocks and herds. This is too much for Pharaoh: no, the male adults only he says – that's what you originally asked for; and he drove Moses and Aaron out of the palace. So Moses stretched forth his rod over the land of Egypt, and Yahweh sent an east wind which brought a devastating plague of locusts. Once again Pharaoh repented, once again Moses was summoned to ask God to withdraw the plague (which he did with a strong west wind), but once again 'Yahweh hardened Pharaoh's heart, so that he would not let the children of Israel go.' The plague of thick darkness follows, and 'they saw not one another, neither rose any from his place for three days: but all the children of Israel had light in their dwellings.' This time, when a desperate Pharaoh summons Moses, there is a change in the Hebrew leader's mood. Earlier we had been shown a touch of ironic humour in his speech: 'And Moses said unto Pharaoh, Glory over me: when shall I entreat for thee, and for thy servants, and for thy people, to destroy the frogs from thee and thy house, that they may remain in the river only?' Then there was a change to the grim scepticism of 9: 30 ('I know that ye will not yet fear Yahweh'). Now, as Moses baits Pharaoh with increasing demands (they must take with them absolutely *everything*, for 'we know not with what we must serve Yahweh, until we come thither') the enraged monarch tells him to get out and never see him again, under penalty of death, to which Moses replies darkly: 'Thou hast spoken well, I will see thy face again no more.'

This is presented as a kind of culmination. After this, the emphasis changes somewhat. There is going to be a final plague, Yahweh tells Moses (11: 1) – it is not yet specified – and then not only will Pharaoh let them go: 'he shall surely thrust you out altogether.' A new theme emerges, that of the out-witting of the Egyptians, who are shown, in contrast to Pharaoh, as favour-ably disposed towards the Israelites. 'Speak now in the ears of the people, and let every man borrow of his neighbour, and every woman of her neighbour, jewels of silver, and jewels of gold. And Yahweh gave the people favour in

The plague of darkness, by Doré.

the sight of the Egyptians. Moreover, the man Moses was very great in the land of Egypt, in the sight of Pharaoh's servants, and in the sight of the people.' The Israelites' borrowing from their Egyptian neighbours (presumably in good faith, though in the circumstances the loans were never repaid) is an obscure element in the story, and seems to be intended to emphasize the good relations between the two groups and hence the isolation of Pharaoh. But this point is not clearly brought out. Indeed, there appears to be some confusion in the presentation of the material in Chapter 11. In verse 4 Moses announces the death of the Egyptian firstborn, but we are not told to whom he is speaking (it is apparently the Israelites). In verse 7 he refers to the children of Israel in the third person, when he says, 'But against any of the children of Israel shall not a dog move his tongue, against man or beast.' By verse 8 he is clearly addressing Pharaoh: 'And all these thy servants shall come down unto me, and bow themselves unto me, saying, Get thee out, and all the people that follow thee: and after that I will go out. And he went out from Pharaoh in a great anger.' We

The last plague, the slaying of the firstborn, by John Martin.

thus suddenly find ourselves in the middle of another confrontation between Moses and Pharaoh which is not properly introduced and which specifically contradicts what Moses had said earlier about seeing Pharaoh's face no more. It looks as though this is another version of the earlier incident.

What follows in Chapter 12 is most interesting. God speaks to Moses and Aaron giving them detailed instructions for the passover sacrifice, using for the first time the phrase 'all the congregation of Israel' (which suggests a later period when they really were a people settled in their own land) and associating the ritual of the passover sacrifice with the means of preventing the slaughter of the Israelite firstborn when God goes forth 'to smite all the firstborn in the land of Egypt, both man and beast'. In 11: 7 it had already been promised that when the Egyptian firstborn were smitten the Israelites would be immune, but here a special rite of protection is prescribed. This is surely an echo of the original passover ritual, a festival of nomadic shepherds at which a sheep or goat was sacrificed and the blood sprinkled to ward off evil powers, which especially threatened the firstborn. The sacrifice of the paschal lamb by each family and the spreading of its blood on the doorposts of the homes of the Israelites so that their firstborn would be spared, reminds us of the 'apotropaic' ('turning away') function of the primitive passover, which seems originally to have been celebrated by nomadic shepherds in the spring on moving from their winter to their summer grazing. What we have here, therefore, is the historicizing of an ancient pastoral ritual by associating it with the slaying of the Egyptian firstborn and the deliverance from Egypt.

Speak ye unto all the congregation of Israel, saying, In the tenth day of this month they shall take to them every man a lamb, according to the house of their fathers, a lamb for a house. And if the household be too little for the lamb, let him and his neighbour next unto his house take it according to the number of souls; every man according to his eating shall make your count for the lamb. . . . And ye shall keep it up until the fourteenth day of the same month: and the whole assembly of the congregation of Israel shall kill it in the evening. And they shall take of the blood, and strike it on the two side posts and on the upper doorpost of the houses, wherein they shall eat it [Exodus 12: 2–7].

The blood of the passover sacrifice will protect the Israelite firstborn. 'And the blood shall be to you for a token upon the houses where ye are: and when I see the blood, I will pass over you, and the plague will not be upon you to destroy you, when I smite the land of Egypt.' The popular derivation of the word 'passover' (translation of the Hebrew *pesach*) derives from this passage:

The death of the firstborn, after Alma-Tadema.

God (or his Angel of Death) passed over (or 'protected') the Israelite house-holds. But in fact the true derivation and the precise meaning of *pesach* remain in doubt, and it is not at all clear what the original name for the nomadic spring sacrifice really signified. But we know that it was taken over in this re-interpretation, plausibly by the historical Moses himself, as a family festival celebrating the deliverance from Egypt. But this is not all. Another ancient festival, that of unleavened bread, was also brought into the picture and associated with the new festival of freedom. This was not a pastoral but an agricultural festival of ancient Palestine in which the first of the grain harvest was ritually consecrated and eaten uncontaminated by the addition of leaven. The injunction to eat unleavened bread for seven days, first found in Exodus 12: 15–20, is presented as something quite distinct from the preceding injunc-tion about the passover sacrifice. These were two ancient and quite separate festivals, each historicized and reinterpreted to serve as a ritual of remem-brance of the deliverance from Egyptian slavery; they were not united into a single festival until a much later period in Israelite history.

OPPOSITE The Israelites sprinkling the blood of the paschal lamb on their doorposts: a 19th-century engraving. BELOW Pharaoh and his courtiers urge Moses to leave Egypt, by Doré.

This sort of thing is very much in keeping with the character and achievement of Moses as it was transmitted through a number of traditions. He rediscovered and reinterpreted his own relationship with his people and his ancestors; he rediscovered and reinterpreted the meaning of Yahweh; and, as we shall see, he was to recast and revitalize traditional bodies of law. The redefinition of two ancient festivals to mark a decisive moment in Israelite history and in the achievement of Israelite identity bears the stamp of the same personality.

And it came to pass, that at midnight Yahweh smote all the firstborn in the land of Egypt, from the firstborn of Pharaoh that sat on his throne unto the firstborn of the captive that was in the dungeon; and all the firstborn of cattle. And Pharaoh rose in the night, he, and all his servants, and all the Egyptians; and there was a great cry in Egypt: for there was not a house where there was not one dead. And he called for Moses and Aaron by night, and said, Rise up, and get you forth from among my people, both ye and the children of Israel; and go, serve Yahweh, as ye have said. Also take your flocks and your herds, as ye have said, and be gone; and bless me also. And the Egyptians were urgent upon the people, that they might send them out of the land in haste; for they said, We be all dead men.

It may not have happened exactly like that, but some fierce and bitter national memory surely lies behind this vivid picture, cruelly triumphant in its grim account of the great mourning cry rising up in Egypt in the night and the now all too human Pharaoh sending in haste for his implacable enemies to give them all they asked, yet curiously elegiac too in its sense of loss and woe and in Pharaoh's almost pathetic plea, 'and bless me also'.

4

Deliverance and After

'And the children of Israel journeyed from Rameses to Succoth, about six hundred thousand on foot that were men, beside children. And a mixed multitude went up also with them; and flocks, and herds, even very much cattle' (Exodus 12: 37–8). Rameses or Raamses, as we have seen, was the residence of the Pharaohs built by Sethos I and Ramesses II in the eastern Nile Delta on the site of the ancient Hyksos capital Avaris. Succoth is a Hebrew form of the Egyptian town name *Tkw*: its ruins are to be found some forty miles south-south-east of Raamses, east of Pithom, on the present Tell el-Maskhuta. The figure of six hundred thousand is clearly impossible. A breakdown by families in Numbers 1 and 26 yields similar figures for men of military age, which suggests that the six hundred thousand in fact represents the active male population of Israel when the account in Numbers was first put together (and even then perhaps inflated). It may have found its way into the story of the exodus as a means of suggesting that all Israel had a share in that crucial historical event, out of which the nation was born. Six hundred thousand males of military age would have meant a total figure of between two and three million, including women and children: it has been pointed out that such a multitude, even if they marched in close order, which they

OVERLEAF The departure of the children of Israel from Egypt: engraving after John Martin.

certainly did not, would have extended from Egypt to Sinai and back (whichever of the proposed sites for Sinai we accept). According to modern scholars, a more realistic figure for those involved in the exodus would be between two and six thousand.

As for the 'mixed multitude' that joined the Israelites in their flight, they were presumably other fugitive slaves who took advantage of this opportunity to seek their freedom; some may have been 'Apiru, and some were apparently Egyptian, if there is any significance in the mention in Leviticus 24: 10 of 'an Israelitish woman whose father was an Egyptian'. Miscellaneous 'Apiru, Egyptian, Midianite and other elements were probably included in this collection of people that Moses led to the mountain of God to be given a new identity as a holy people with a special covenant with Yahweh and an obligation to abide by the ethical and ritual code prescribed by him. That all of those who became the people of Israel were descended from the twelve sons of Jacob and their families who settled in Egypt (seventy souls in all, we are told in Genesis 46: 27) is a national myth that developed later for understandable reasons. And while we cannot accept it literally, it does preserve a central truth: Israel as a whole owed to Moses and to the events associated with his name its emergence as a nation with a sense of its own identity.

'And they baked unleavened cakes of the dough which they brought forth out of Egypt, for it was not leavened; because they were thrust out of Egypt, and could not tarry, neither had they prepared for themselves any victuals.' (Exodus 12: 39.) We have already been told in verse 33 that 'the people took their dough before it was leavened, their kneading-troughs being bound up in their clothes upon their shoulders', and now we get the clear suggestion the eating of unleavened bread was because they had not time to bake proper leavened bread. Three strands in the narrative of the Mosaic books are attributed by scholars to three different writers whom they call J, P and E. This attempt to explain the combination of the passover sacrifice (additional instructions for which follow immediately in verses 43–9) and the feast of unleavened bread is generally attributed to the writer J, who is interested in reasonable and humanly understandable explanations (while P is much more interested in cultic ordinances and the divine purpose). We may well suppose that the fusion of the two feasts was not Moses' doing, but that it came later under the impact of the memory of the exodus and the coincidence of dates. Moses' interest we may plausibly conjecture to have been centred on the passover sacrifice as a community celebration (observed by individual families but with a driving sense of participating in a communal act) emphasizing the

The passover: from a medieval illustrated Haggadah.

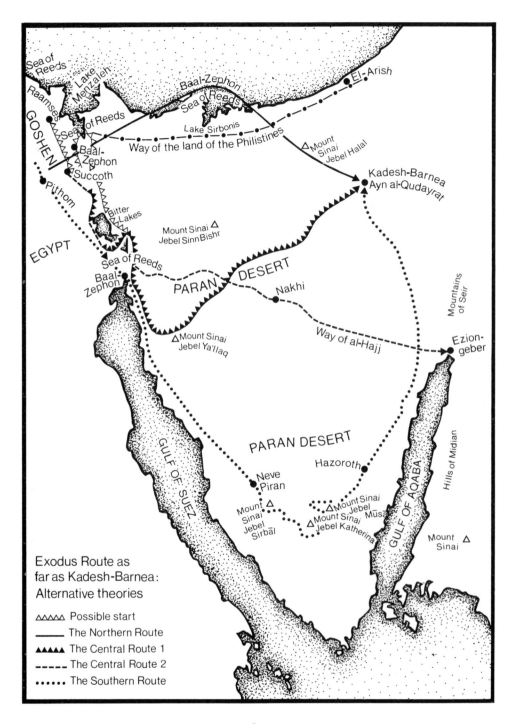

Exodus Route as
far as Kadesh-Barnea:
Alternative theories

△△△△△ Possible start
⎯⎯⎯ The Northern Route
▲▲▲▲▲ The Central Route 1
----- The Central Route 2
••••• The Southern Route

emerging sense of unity and purpose among the celebrators. Again and again we find in the Moses traditions evidence of his proceeding by way of reinterpreting existing ritual, customs, even language. As Buber put it, here 'he transformed the existent Passover by introducing a new sense and symbol, as Jesus did later by the introduction of a new sense and symbol.' When we come to look at the laws associated with Moses and their analogues in other codes of the ancient Near East, we shall find a similar pattern. The Moses traditions never show him as making a clean break with the past. Although the giving of the Law on Mount Sinai is presented as a unique and history-making event, the God who delivers his commandments on the mountain has already been identified by Moses as the God of the fathers. Revolutionary ideas are presented in the language of tradition or are inserted into the midst of traditional material. (It is all, one might say, very English: something similar happened in England in the seventeenth century.)

Further evidence of the determined linking of the passover sacrifice and the feast of unleavened bread with the exodus and the birth of the Israelite nation is found in Exodus 13: 1–16. The writer looks to the future, sees the people settled in the Promised Land, and prescribes (as orders given by Yahweh to Moses for delivery to the people) commemorative ceremonies and rituals for perpetual observance. Here as in the concluding verses of the previous chapter the background of the instructions is not the circumstances of the people as they were preparing to leave Egypt, but a settled agricultural way of life. At this critical point in the story of the exodus all the traditions concerning its later commemoration were brought together by the redactor who produced these passages, which appear to be relatively late. That the regulations were said to be mediated by Moses is a tribute to the strength of the tradition that we shall meet with so often, that Moses was *the* transmitter of Israelite cultic as well as ethical ordinances and that these came to him from Yahweh.

When the Israelites and the others left Egypt, 'God led them not through the ways of the land of the Philistines, although that was near; for God said, Lest peradventure the people repent when they see war, and they return to Egypt.' It has been argued that the mention of the Philistines is an anachronism, since it was only at the beginning of the twelfth century BC (by which time the Israelites were well settled in Palestine) that the Philistines began to settle on the Palestinian coastal plain. But however this may be, there were certainly strongly fortified cities there at this time. Further, the approach to Egypt from the coastal plain to the east was guarded by Egyptian forces stationed in fortresses, with whom a confrontation had to be avoided. So the tradition that Moses led the people a long way round to avoid such a confrontation seems well founded, even though the exact route followed remains a matter of conjecture. We are told that they 'journeyed from Succoth, and encamped in Etham, in the edge of the wilderness'. Etham, which presumably represents a Hebrew form of an Egyptian place-name, remains unidentified. One thing, however, we can say for certain: the sea to which they travelled and which the Authorized Version translates as the Red Sea was not the Red Sea at all. The Hebrew words, *yam suf*, mean 'sea of reeds' (or even 'papyrus marsh'). Since the land of Goshen, where the Hebrews were settled, was 'the land of Rameses' (Genesis 47: 11) in the Eastern Delta region, it would be plausible that they should have moved eastward across an arm of Lake Menzaleh, or that they should have gone further eastward along the coast and crossed a corner of Lake Sirbonis. Both of these bodies of water would merit the name Sea of Reeds. On the other hand, these routes, especially the latter, would have taken them into 'the way of the land of the Philistines' which we are specifically told they avoided. Did they move due south immediately after crossing Lake Menzaleh, keeping to the eastern side of the Bitter Lakes and the Gulf of Suez? Or did they move south and cross one of the Bitter Lakes between the Gulf of Suez and the Eastern Delta? This too would have been a 'sea of reeds'. Or did they move further south, to Baal-Zephon (possibly modern Jebel 'Atāqa) at the top of the Gulf of Suez, crossing an extreme northern corner of that Gulf? The fact is that the traditions that have come down to us in Exodus about the movements of the children of Israel in the wilderness are too confused and represent too many different strands to allow of any definite sorting out of the historical base. Those who argue that the Sea of Reeds was the Sirbonian Sea cite Exodus 14: 2 ('Speak unto the children of Israel, that they turn back and encamp before Pi-hahiroth, between Migdol and the sea, over against Baal-zephon: before it ye shall encamp by the sea') and, locating Baal-Zephon on the northern arm of Lake Sirbonis, argue from the specificity of the topography that this represents a very old and possibly authentic local tradition to be preferred to the other, and less specific, traditions about the group's movements. This would mean dismissing the warning against going 'by the way of the Philistines' as later and undependable. But this is a minority view. The present writer believes on the whole that the evidence, doubtful though it is, tends rather to support the view that they moved south-east from Raamses to Succoth, then, pursued by the Egyptians, moved north-north-east to Lake Menzaleh, the narrow southern part of which they crossed before turning south to proceed along the eastern side of the Gulf of Suez.

We are dealing with traditions cherished and handed down by people transmitting in the most solemn way their view of their own origins, not with history as such. What is important is what remained engraved on the national memory. When we read therefore at the end of Exodus 13 of the divine

ABOVE The defeat of Pharaoh's army, from a 13th-century psalter.

OVERLEAF The crossing of the Red Sea, by Raphael.

guidance out of Egypt, we are struck by the power of the symbols used and the rhythmic, almost incantatory force of the language, which comes across even in English translation. (That translation, as elsewhere in this book, is normally the Authorized or King James Version, except that frequently, for reasons made clear in Chapter 2, the tetragrammaton is rendered 'Yahweh' rather than 'the Lord'.)

And Yahweh went before them by day in a pillar of cloud, to lead them the
way; and by night in a pillar of fire, to give them light; to go by day and night.

He took not away the pillar of the cloud by day, nor the pillar of fire by night,
from before the people.

The assurance of divine protection, so central in the exodus story, pulses
through the language. Did the symbols of cloud and fire come from memories
of an erupting volcano? There are no volcanic mountains on the Sinai
peninsula, and to find one we would have to go to the eastern side of the Gulf
of Aqaba. Some scholars have indeed taken the wandering Israelites to north-
western Arabia and located Mount Sinai there, but it is scarcely necessary to be
so literal in pursuit of the cloud and fire, even if the distance involved did not in
any case make this theory highly improbable. Some ancient memory of a
volcanic eruption may indeed have been handed down and found its way
into this account of the symbols of God's presence. It is even conceivable that
the Kenites, who were desert smiths and would therefore carry fire about
with them and whom the biblical story associates closely with Moses, were
able to produce smoke and fire which came to be looked on and remembered
as some kind of divine sign. Or perhaps the smoke of sacrifice ascending at a
sanctuary played some part in the development of the cloud image. The
important thing is that to the imagination of the people of Israel the cloud and
the fire were an assurance of God's presence and of Moses' divinely authenti-
cated role as leader of the people to a new destiny.

'And it was told the king of Egypt that the people fled' (Exodus 14: 5). This
seems to be a different tradition from the one recorded earlier, that Pharaoh
actually threw them out. It is certainly a more plausible explanation of his
pursuit of them, for if he had evicted them he could not have regarded them as
illegal fugitives. The narrator, however, smoothes over any apparent in-
consistency by telling us that once again Pharaoh changed his mind. He
decided to pursue the people of Israel with his war chariots. The war chariot
had been introduced into Egypt by the Hyksos and at the time of the New
Kingdom was the principal feature of the Egyptian fighting forces. So
Pharaoh 'took six hundred chosen chariots, and all the chariots of Egypt, and
captains over every one of them' and pursued the children of Israel. Now it is
interesting that the Hebrew word here translated 'captains' is *shalishim*, which
literally means 'third men'. In fact the Egyptians fought with two men to a
chariot, one to drive and one to fight: it was the Hittite-Palestinian method to
have three men to a chariot, the third acting as aid and shield-bearer to the
fighter, and these war chariots did not come into use with the Israelite army
until the time of Solomon. So we see the narrator setting down the tradition
that had come down to him in terms appropriate to the world he knew.

Hamam Far'aoun, 'the hot waters of Pharaoh', on the western edge of the Sinai desert and the east bank of the Gulf of Suez. Here the Egyptian chariots are supposed to have been bogged.

When the children of Israel saw Pharaoh's host approaching, they were terrified, and cried out to the Lord. They also reproached Moses, saying to him: 'Because there were no graves in Egypt, hast thou taken us away to die in the wilderness?' (Exodus 14: 11). This is the grimmest kind of irony, and sounds absolutely authentic: Egypt was of course positively obsessed with graves; their famous pyramids were the graves of the Pharaohs and their whole religion was oriented towards death and elaborate tombs. The question is pure black humour. They go on to complain – was it the 'mixed multitude', feeling perhaps more Egyptian and less Israelite than the others, who led the complaints? – that they would have been better off if they had stayed in Egypt and to reproach Moses for having led them out. This is a recurring theme in the story of Moses and emphasizes the problems of leadership that he faced and overcame. It was not an easy matter to create a nation out of a bunch of fugitive slaves.

Moses' reply to the people's complaints, as given in Exodus 14: 13–14, presents him as absolutely confident of divine help in repelling the pursuing Egyptians. 'And Moses said unto the people, Fear ye not, stand still, and see the salvation of Yahweh, which he will show to you today: for the Egyptians

91

whom ye have seen today, ye shall see them again no more for ever. Yahweh shall fight for you, and ye shall hold your peace.' And then we are told of Yahweh's command to Moses to lift up his rod and stretch his hand over the sea, to divide the waters, so that the children of Israel could 'go on dry ground through the midst of the sea'. The record of the actual occurrence, which seems to conflate two traditions, certainly testifies to an enormous sense of divine deliverance:

And the children of Israel went into the midst of the sea upon the dry ground: and the waters were a wall unto them on their right hand, and on their left. And the Egyptians pursued and went in after them to the midst of the sea, even all Pharaoh's horses, his chariots, and his horsemen [i.e., charioteers]. And it came to pass, that in the morning watch Yahweh looked unto the host of the Egyptians through the pillar of fire and of the cloud, and troubled the host of the Egyptians. And took off their chariot wheels, that they drave them heavily: so that the Egyptians said, Let us flee from the face of Israel; for Yahweh fighteth for them against the Egyptians.

And Yahweh said unto Moses, Stretch out thine hand over the sea, that the waters may come upon the Egyptians, upon their chariots, and upon their horsemen. And Moses stretched forth his hand over the sea, and the sea returned to his strength when the morning appeared; and the Egyptians fled into it; and Yahweh overthrew the Egyptians in the midst of the sea. And the waters returned, and covered the chariots, and the horsemen, and all the host of Pharaoh that came into the sea after them; there remained not so much as one of them. But the children of Israel walked upon dry land in the midst of the sea; and the waters were a wall unto them on their right hand, and on their left [Exodus 14: 22–9].

At the beginning of this account we are told that the children of Israel crossed the sea that had been specially divided for them, with walls of water piled up on either side. The Egyptians pursued. We are also told that Yahweh took off their chariot wheels, which suggests that the Egyptian war chariots got stuck in the mud. A more mysterious note (the writer here is assumed to be J) emerges in the account of Yahweh's looking forth upon the Egyptian army through the pillar of fire and of cloud, and as a result the Egyptians flee in terror into the sea. (The Authorized Version rendering 'and the Egyptians fled against it', is clearly wrong: it should be 'the Egyptians fled *into* it'.) If the Egyptians were caught by a returning tide, with their chariot wheels bogged down in the marshy ground, this would support the view that the action took place at Lake Sirbonis, the incoming tide coming in swiftly over the mud-flats to trap the mired Egyptians. But though we may be able to see traces of different versions of the story of deliverance – the Egyptians being driven into the sea through fear of Yahweh, the Egyptians overwhelmed by a returning tide, or a simply miraculous division of the waters for the children of Israel and the piled up waters collapsing on to the Egyptians after the children of Israel had got across – the theme that emerges is clear and strong: an army of Egyptian war chariots was destroyed in or beside a body of water in an unexpected and remarkable way. This much must have a historical base. The fact that no such Egyptian disaster is mentioned in Egyptian records is no argument against this: the Egyptians never recorded their defeats.

Further evidence of the genuineness of the tradition is the song of triumph recorded in Exodus 15. This is the earliest preserved Hebrew poem of any length, and it is considerably earlier than the prose account in the midst of which it is set. The opening two lines (which also constitute the 'song of Miriam' in verse 21) represent a very ancient hymn of triumph and deliverance from an army of charioteers at the sea:

> I will sing unto Yahweh, for he is highly exalted:
> The horse and his charioteer hath he thrown into the sea.

Parallels have been found between the structure and imagery of this poem and the structure and imagery of ancient Ugaritic poems to Baal. The first part describes with great vividness the destruction of the Egyptian army, and the second half, at least some verses of which must be of a later date, describes the dread that falls on the inhabitants of Canaan when the children of Israel arrive to take possession of their Promised Land. Yet even this second part, which mentions events which took place in later generations and refers anachronistically to the discomfiture of the Philistines, includes some very ancient phrases which can be paralleled in other ancient Semitic literature. For example, verse 17 runs:

> Thou shalt bring it [the people] in and plant it
> In the mountain of thy inheritance,

which some scholars have taken to be a reference to the Second Temple and therefore late sixth century in date; but it has been shown by Albright to be precisely parallel to the Baal Epic of Ugarit, in which Baal refers to Mount Zaphon as 'the mountain of mine inheritance' using the identical word for 'inheritance'. The reference therefore is not to the Second Temple but to the holy mountain that plays such a significant part in the exodus story. Rhythms and patterns similarly show parallels with ancient Canaanite poetry, as in the *abc–abd* pattern of verse 6:

> Thy right hand, Yahweh, is glorious in power.
> Thy right hand, Yahweh, dasheth in pieces the enemy.

Miriam by W. Hensel.

So, although this great Reed Sea Hymn must have been modified in the course
of its transmission and shows references to events that occurred later (such as
the amazement and dread that fell upon the leaders of Edom and Moab (verse
15), which refers to the detour to be made by Israel through southern Transjordan before entering the Promised Land), it is essentially a very ancient song
of triumph written in a literary form much older than the prose narrative that
surrounds it. To give the modern English reader a sense of how it emerges
from its Hebrew context it would have to be rendered in, say, a rough imita-
tion of the old alliterative Anglo-Saxon heroic style. It would then read something like this (which is a paraphrase rather than a literal translation):

I will make a song to Yahweh   mighty in majesty
Horse and his charioteer   he has hurled into the sea.
Yahweh is my strength   my stronghold is he also,
My doughty deliverer   he has declared himself.
He is my God   and glory will I give him,
My father's God   and I will flaunt his praises.
Confident in combat   Yahweh is he called.
The doughtiest drivers   dearest to Pharaoh
The train of his troops   he has tumbled in the tide;
Silent under sea   they are sunk like a stone.
Thy right hand, Yahweh,   high-raised and heavenly,
The shock of thy shaft   hath scattered the foe.
Mighty in majesty   thou hast mangled thine enemies,
Discharging thine anger   thou has consumed them like chaff.
In the rush of thy rage   raised were the waters
Far down in the depths   they were drawn to a heap.
Confident the foeman   for conquest and capture,
Boastful in talking   bold in his blood-lust.
Thou didst blow with thy blast   they were borne to the bottom,
Plummeting low   they were lodged in the seabed.
Who like our Lord   hath such might among leaders,
What other hero   so holy and high?
Praise him for his power   the performer of wonders.
Thy hand is thrust outward   the earth hath engulfed them.

In thy love hast thou led them   thy people delivered,
In thy strength thou hast helped them   to thy holy habitation.
The nations took note   they trembled with terror,
Those who dwell in Philistia   were frenzied with fear.
Then the Edomite chieftains   were chilled with amazement,
Mute in misgiving   were the mighty of Moab,
And all those in Canaan   confused and cast down.
Dread and dismay   descended upon them,
By thy arm's lordly strength   they stayed silent as stone
While thine own people, Yahweh,   passed peacefully over,
Thy people passed over   whom thou hast protected.
Thou shalt lead them and lodge them   in thine own lofty places,
In dear divine dwelling   that thou didst devise.
Yahweh reigns ever   eternally lasting.

The point is that someone reading it at the time when it was first incorporated into the narrative would be conscious at once of reading something in a very early poetic style.

In Exodus 15: 21 we are told that 'Miriam the prophetess, the sister of Aaron, took a timbrel in her hand; and all the women went out after her with timbrels and with dances.' And they sang the Reed Sea Victory Hymn. Ancient though the hymn is, the account of Miriam singing it here is given in terms of later custom. In the circumstances of the exodus, with the whole body of people moving together, it is quite unrealistic to present the women as coming out to greet the returning warriors after their victory. This, of course, was the custom after Israel had been settled in the Promised Land. 'And it came to pass as they came, when David was returned from the slaughter of the Philistine, that the women came out of all cities of Israel, singing and dancing, to meet king Saul, with tabrets, with joy, and with instruments of music' (I Samuel 18: 6).

Ever afterwards the Israelites looked back on their successful crossing of the Reed Sea and their shaking off the Egyptians as the decisive victory. To them, in Martin Noth's words, 'the events at the sea were so unique and extraordinary that it came to constitute the essence of the primary Israelite confession and was regarded as the real beginning of Israel's history and the act of God fundamental for Israel.' A miracle has been described as an event which creates faith: it might equally be described as the retrospective redefinition of an event in the light of faith.

'So Moses brought Israel from the Reed Sea, and they went out into the wilderness of Shur; and they went three days in the wilderness and found no water.' We do not know where Shur is. In Genesis 25: 18 it is said to be 'before Egypt, as thou goest toward Assyria', and in I Samuel 15: 7 it is described as 'over against Egypt'. It must have been somewhere in the north-eastern Sinai peninsula, facing Egypt's eastern border. Accompanied as they were by their flocks of sheep and goats, as well as donkeys, the wanderers needed regular and abundant supplies of water in their journeyings. The search for water is a recurring theme in the biblical account of the Israelites' years in the wilderness. In the wilderness of Shur they found water, but it was bitter and undrinkable (not surprising in the salty ground of the wilderness), 'and the people murmured against Moses'. Yahweh shows Moses how to sweeten the water by casting a certain tree into it – presumably an echo of a genuine process of making brackish water drinkable by the addition of certain herbs. But the point of the story lies in the people's fickleness and Moses' resourcefulness. The biblical account of the people's murmuring against Moses comes immediately after the hymn of victory for deliverance at the Reed Sea, as though to emphasize that even the most impressive displays of divine help cannot be

Brackish water at Marah. Nowadays it is a rich source of salt, on evaporation, for the Bedouin.

counted on to stifle the voice of complaint. That voice is raised again and again throughout the whole period of wandering in the wilderness, and again and again Moses is hard put to it to find a satisfactory response. Sometimes he is shown as ready to give up; at other times, God is shown as ready to give up, and Moses dissuades him. What comes through strongly in these traditions is Moses' patience, endurance and sheer genius as a leader.

They come to Elim (unidentifiable), where there is abundant water. Then they come 'unto the wilderness of Sin, which is between Elim and Sinai, on the fifteenth day of the second month, after their departing out of the land of Egypt'. Where was Moses leading them? To Mount Sinai, the holy mountain, for the enactment of a solemn covenant with Yahweh and the proclamation of Yahweh's commands. We do not know which mountain was Mount Sinai. If we did, we might be able to place the wilderness of Sin with confidence, and if we knew exactly what was meant by the wilderness of Sin (is it in fact just a variation of the name 'Sinai'?) we would be in a better position to locate the mountain. If we believe that the Israelites took the eastward route past Lake Sirbonis and along the shore, we could identify Mount Sinai with Jebel al-Halāl in the north–western part of the Sinai peninsula, west of Kadesh-

97

barnea. If we think they crossed one of the Bitter Lakes we could see Jebel
Sinn-Bishr as Mount Sinai, or perhaps Jebel Ya'allaq further south. If we
believe that the Israelites pushed their way south down the eastern side of the
Gulf of Suez before turning west and then north, we could locate Mount
Sinai at Jebel Sirbāl, Jebel Mūsā or Jebel Katherina. Some even put it on the
eastern side of the Gulf of Aqaba. A site in the southern Sinai peninsula seems
on the whole most likely, perhaps Jebel Katherina, which is supported by a
tradition dating from the early Christian period and which is near the
Egyptian copper mines of Serābît el-Khâdim, thus fitting in well with the
biblical tradition that Moses' Kenite relatives (and the Kenites, it will be
remembered, were smiths) were found in the area. There can, however, be
no certainty in the matter. But we can be certain in a general way of what
happened to the people of Israel at that place, wherever it was.

We are told that they came to the wilderness of Sin 'on the fifteenth day of
the second month after their departing out of the land of Egypt', that is a
month and a half after they first set out. We need not expect the writer (presumed here to be P) to relate his chronology to his mileage in any detailed way;
whether he supposed the people to have spent quite a long time at Elim or to

Wadi Firan, possibly the site of Elim, the fruitful oasis the Israelites reached with relief.

98

have stopped at several other places he does not trouble to mention, the fact is that he is hastening to his account of the second 'murmuring' of the people against Moses, this time because of the inadequate diet in the wilderness. 'Would we had died by the hand of Yahweh in the land of Egypt, when we sat by the fleshpots, and when we did eat bread to the full; for ye have brought us forth into this wilderness, to kill this whole assembly with hunger.' They probably romanticized in retrospect their diet as Egyptian slaves: it cannot have been particularly abundant. But it was probably true that the life of wanderers in the wilderness was in many ways more difficult than the life of slaves in Egypt, especially when those slaves lived as a separate community in their own part of the country with their own flocks and herds.

The hungry Israelites are fed with quails and the mysterious substance called manna, but not before Moses has warned the people that it is Yahweh they are murmuring against, not Aaron and himself, and implies that Yahweh's plan for the people is not necessarily that of the people of Israel. The quails came up in the evening, and here are only mentioned as arriving on one occasion, while the manna is discovered lying on the ground every morning after the dew had gone. Quails are brought in again in Chapter 11 of Numbers,

Typical wilderness terrain in the southern Sinai peninsula.

99

ABOVE Jebel Mūsā, one of the suggested sites of Mount Sinai. OPPOSITE Serābît el-Khâdim, where the Kenites mined copper.

in a rather more desperate situation when Moses is on the brink of giving up his responsibility for the people in exasperation: the account in Exodus is apparently a putting together once and for all of all the traditions of miraculous feeding in the wilderness available to the narrator. The main interest of the narrator here is in the manna, which is described in such explicit detail that it looks as though he is identifying it with a substance of which he himself has personal knowledge. Some modern scholars confidently identify manna with a substance produced by two varieties of coccidae (scale insects) when they extract sap from the branches of the tamarisk (a shrub native to the wilderness), *Tamarix mannifera*, and secrete it in the form of drops of transparent liquid that congeal into white globules composed of glucose, fructose and a little pectin. These globules fall from the leaves on to the ground, where they harden in the cool of the night. They dissolve when the sun comes up, so they must be gathered in the early morning. They are said to be still eaten with pleasure by nomadic inhabitants of the inland region of the Sinai peninsula and to be called *mann* by them. All this fits exactly the biblical account of manna and the instructions for gathering and eating it. The explanation of the word given in Exodus (from the Hebrew *man hu*, meaning both 'what is it?' – which would properly be *mah hu* in Hebrew – and 'it is *man*'), if it is indeed meant as an explanation, is pure folk etymology. As for the quails, which 'came up and covered the camp' (Exodus 16: 13) or which were brought in by a wind from the sea (Numbers 11: 31), some commentators have taken their appearance to support the view that the Israelites wandered near the

100

RIGHT The tamarisk, from which the Israelites possibly collected manna. BELOW Manna falling from heaven, from a 12th-century Byzantine Bible.

Mediterranean coast, since these migratory birds regularly come there; others say that they are commonest in the region of the Red Sea. But the killing and eating of birds in the wilderness would seem to be plausible activities not necessarily linked to any particular one of the many suggested alternative routes.

It is interesting that the first reference to the sabbath in the Old Testament occurs in the instructions Moses issues (as always, in the name of Yahweh) about the handling of manna: on the sixth day of the week they must gather twice as much so that it will be sufficient also for the following day, which is 'the rest of the holy sabbath unto Yahweh' (Exodus 16: 23). Now the sabbath is not introduced here as something wholly new, for it is referred to at the beginning of verse 23 as something about which Yahweh had previously spoken. Here again Moses is presented as renewing and reinterpreting an old institution. The special significance of the seventh day is already present in the creation story as told in Chapter 1 of Genesis: God created the world in six days and rested on the seventh. 'And God blessed the seventh day, and sanctified it: because that in it he had rested from all his work which he had made' (Genesis 2: 3). Seven was a holy number in ancient Mesopotamian culture and in the Babylonian Creation Epic, *Enūma elish* ('When on High'), which follows exactly the same course of events as we find in the opening chapter of Genesis and the first verses of the second chapter, the gods rest and celebrate on the seventh day after having completed the work of creation. It is likely that some form of sabbath had been celebrated by Semitic peoples long before Moses. What we find about the sabbath in connection with the accounts of lawgiving by Moses emphasizes on the one hand its supernatural and cosmic character (the extra manna gathered on the sixth day miraculously stayed fresh on the seventh, but a double amount gathered on a weekday went bad) and on the other its human, social purpose. In Exodus 16: 23 it is 'a holy sabbath unto Yahweh' and when this is embodied in the fourth commandment it is described as 'a sabbath unto Yahweh thy God' in which not only must every man rest but all his family and all his servants must rest too. Here the reason given is 'for in six days Yahweh made heaven and earth, the sea, and all that in them is, and rested the seventh day: wherefore Yahweh blessed the sabbath day, and hallowed it' (Exodus 20: 10–11). In Exodus 31: 15 Moses again announces, in Yahweh's name, that 'the seventh day is the sabbath of rest, holy to Yahweh'. In the recapitulation of the Ten Commandments found in Chapter 5 of Deuteronomy, after the specific prohibition of work on the sabbath on the part of all members of the family, their servants, their animals and 'the stranger that is within thy gate', there is a specific humanitarian reason added: 'that thy manservant and thy maidservant may rest as well as thou'; and then, instead of the reminder of God's creation of the world in six days and resting on the seventh, we get the injunction: 'And remember that thou wast a servant in the land of Egypt, and that Yahweh thy God brought thee out thence through a mighty arm: therefore Yahweh thy God commanded thee to keep the sabbath day.' The traditions about the sabbath as redefined by Moses thus combine the divine and the human, the cosmic and the historical, the cultic and the ethical, the ritual and the humanitarian. Though there can be little doubt that a great number of later cultic and other injunctions had already been incorporated in the Mosaic law by the time it was presented in the biblical books of Moses, we can nevertheless recognize the hand of Moses in this dual definition of the origin and purpose of the sabbath. Divine laws imply something about the relation of God to the universe and also about the relation of individual man to society. We shall see more of this Mosaic duality.

Quails falling from heaven: from a 13th-century German chronicle.

5

The Mountain of God

We are told in the opening of Chapter 17 of Exodus that when the children of Israel reached Rephidim (a place not certainly identifiable) and pitched their camp there, they found no water to drink and they complained to Moses. 'Wherefore is this that thou hast brought us up out of Egypt, to kill us and our children and our cattle with thirst?' This, as we have seen, is not the first nor is to be the last of the people's 'murmurings' against their leader when things are not going well with them, and it may well be that some of the accounts represent variant versions of the same tradition rather than different incidents that occurred consecutively. Numbers 20: 3–11 presents an almost identical story. Both here and in Exodus 17 Moses appeals to Yahweh and is instructed how to get water from the rock. In the Exodus story he is told to strike the rock with his rod and does so: water gushes forth. 'And he called the name of the place Massah, and Meribah, because of the chiding of the children of Israel, and because they tempted Yahweh, saying, Is Yahweh with us or not?' The Hebrew *massah* means 'tempting' or 'proving' and *meribah* means 'chiding' or 'strife'. But the true etymology of Meribah is more likely to be from *rib* in the sense of a legal dispute rather than strife; it was probably a name given by nomadic shepherds to a spring by which they assembled to settle their disputes. It may well have been known to the Israelites in later times, and associated with the desert miracle by the almost miraculous abundance of the gushing water in a dry land. Massah must have been a different place. Meribah is mentioned again, with Massah, in the Numbers story, and Massah is mentioned by itself twice in Deuteronomy (6: 16 and 9: 22) as a place where the Israelites 'tempted' or 'provoked' Yahweh. Particular desert springs were probably long associated by tradition with the wandering in the wilderness and their names interpreted in terms of the combined traditions of the shortage of water and the murmurings against Moses. What concerns us here is the evidence of Moses' repeated difficulty in keeping the people contented and firm of purpose during their arduous journey. 'What shall I do unto this people? They be almost ready to stone me,' he exclaims to Yahweh in near-despair. Yahweh reassures him and tells him what to do. The meaning of this is clear enough: Moses intermittently loses the people's confidence but on each occasion his resilience, determination and faith bring him out on top in the end. Neither the children of Israel nor Moses are idealized in this account. The former are stiffnecked and ungrateful; the latter, for all his charisma, has no automatic sway over those he leads. For an account of a people marching to a tremendous rendezvous with history, the theophany at Mount Sinai which will ever after be cherished by them as an unparalleled and epoch-making experience, it is curiously stumbling and hesitant. The journeyings in the wilderness are not presented as an epic of heroic endurance in the face of enormous obstacles, but as a series of accounts of grumblings, weakness of will and loss of faith. The people are ready enough to believe in Yahweh and follow Moses in moments of obvious deliverance, but if Yahweh cannot give them success in everything right away they assume that his mediator Moses is not performing his function properly. But there is another point implicit in these traditions. A people that has been delivered from the power of a despot to become an independent group wandering on their own is not likely to accept tamely the authority of any new leader. Having learned to hate despotism, they are suspicious of any form of authority. They will take nothing on trust. Everything must be demonstrated. (The Americans attribute a similar attitude to the inhabitants of Missouri, who always say, 'Show me'.) Nomadic life in the desert breeds (as it still does) its own kind of democracy, of suspicion of absolute authority. And though this may produce grumbling and scepticism, it has its positive side. Can some such notion be implied in the stories of 'murmuring' that are recorded in the Moses traditions? What certainly comes across is the difficulty of Moses' task in leading this stubborn people to a new destiny, and the tenacity and endurance he displayed in accomplishing it.

Another view of Jebel Mūsā and the surrounding area.

'Then came Amalek, and fought with Israel in Rephidim' (Exodus 17: 8). It is probable that the words 'in Rephidim' have slipped in from verse 1 of this chapter and do not really belong here, for if the confederacy of nomadic tribes known as the Amalekites were attacking in order to prevent Israelite penetration into Palestine from the south it must have been at a later stage in their wanderings. But, as so often, much depends on which theory we adopt about the route they took. At any rate it seems likely that the battle with the Amalekites took place in the northern part of the Sinai peninsula and the mention of specific topographical details suggests that the place was still known when the account was put into its biblical form ('the top of the hill' is twice mentioned). Joshua suddenly appears here for the first time with no explanation, as a military leader whom Moses puts in command of the Israelite army in its fight against the Amalekites. Moses plays a different part: he goes to the top of the hill, with Aaron and Hur, and holds up his hand. 'And it came to pass, when Moses held up his hand, that Israel prevailed; and when he let down his hand, Amalek prevailed.' (The change from the singular 'hand' in verse 9 to the plural 'hands' in verse 12 is clearly a mistake: the attitude is not

Moses strikes water from the rock: from a medieval German chronicle.

one of prayer but one of guidance and command. We are told that in his hand is his rod, which from his advantageous position on the hilltop he could use to signal the movements of the enemy to Joshua below.) The Amalekites were defeated. 'And Yahweh said unto Moses, Write this for a memorial, and rehearse it in the ears of Joshua: for I will utterly blot out the remembrance of Amalek from under heaven.' This is one of the very few occasions when Moses is told to write an actual part of the narrative in the biblical books associated with his name. It is evidence of the special animus against the Amalekites, which is in some measure explained and further illustrated by Deuteronomy 25: 17–19:

Remember what Amalek did unto thee by the way, when ye were come forth out of Egypt, how he met thee by the way, and smote the hindmost of thee, even all that were feeble behind thee, when thou wast faint and weary; and he feared not God. Therefore it shall be, when Yahweh thy God hath given thee rest from all thine enemies round about, in the land which Yahweh thy God giveth thee for an inheritance to possess it, that thou shalt blot out the remembrance of Amalek from under heaven; thou shalt not forget.

The tradition here preserved is that Amalek attacked and destroyed a weary, straggling rearguard that was cut off from the main body of Israelites, and just as Henry v became enraged (according to Shakespeare) when the French before Agincourt attacked the tents of his army in the rear and slew the boy attendants there, so Moses became enraged and ordered Joshua to lead a body of Israelites against Amalek when the latter was dividing the spoils and thought he was safe. To attack a weak and weary rearguard was not in the tradition of the warfare of the time; it showed, as the Deuteronomist put it, a lack of fear of God. It was a vicious and cowardly attack, memory of which the Israelites conscientiously preserved. (The paradox of their being enjoined never to forget to blot out remembrance of Amalek presumably illustrates the strength of the emotion that produced the injunction.) The victory over Amalek is solemnized by the account of Moses building an altar and calling it 'Yahweh is my banner'. He then makes a formal declaration of the eternal war between Amalek and Yahweh (and here we cannot accept the Authorized Version rendering but give a literal translation of the Hebrew): 'Hand on throne, Yah! ['Yah' is an abbreviation for 'Yahweh'.] Yahweh will war against Amalek from generation to generation.' That is, Moses asks Yahweh to swear with his hand on his throne to keep fighting for Israel against Amalek. (It may be that the Hebrew word translated 'throne', *kes* – which is unusual, as the regular form is *kisse* – should be read as *nes*, banner or flagpole, and that the first part of Moses' pronouncement should be rendered: 'The hand on the flagpole of Yah!' But the general sense is unaltered.)

At this point in the Exodus narrative Jethro is reintroduced. He comes 'unto Moses in the wilderness where he was encamped at the mount of God' bringing with him Moses' wife and two sons. 'And Moses told his father-in-law all that Yahweh had done unto Pharaoh and to the Egyptians for Israel's sake, and all the travail that had come upon them by the way, and how Yahweh delivered them.' The account stresses the cordiality of the relations between Moses and his father-in-law and Jethro's pleasure at Israel's deliverance.

And Jethro said, Blessed be Yahweh, who hath delivered you out of the hand of the Egyptians, and out of the hand of Pharaoh. . . . Now I know that Yahweh is greater than all the gods: for in the thing wherein they dealt proudly he was above them. And Jethro, Moses' father-in-law, took a burnt offering and sacrificed to God [Elohim]: and Aaron came, and all the elders of Israel, to eat bread with Moses' father-in-law before God.

This passage has given rise to a long debate among scholars as to whether Jethro was now converted to a belief in the omnipotence of Yahweh or whether, as Yahweh was already the God of the Kenites, he was merely rejoicing in this exhibition of Yahweh's powers and in Israel's good fortune at having secured Yahweh's special protection. Or perhaps Yahweh had previously been *a* god of the Kenites and is now seen to be *the* God. Clearly some tradition of a historical relationship between Israelites and Kenites is at work here, but it is not easy to identify it precisely. In this chapter Jethro is referred to as Moses' father-in-law eleven times, which suggests that the narrator is anxious to stress the family relationship between the two. But Jethro is also referred to in the opening verse as 'the priest of Midian'. And it is Jethro who apparently presides over the sacrifice to God and the subsequent ritual meal that follow his profession of faith in Yahweh. The significance of the sacrifice being described as offered to Elohim and not to Yahweh is obscure; but it is clear that to Jethro here, as to the narrator throughout, Elohim *is* Yahweh. Is this what Jethro has now realized? Or has he realized that the god or gods whom he had previously worshipped are now subsumed in the single all-powerful Yahweh? (When he exclaims 'Now I know that Yahweh is greater than all the gods', the word for gods is *elohim*, this time used as the plural which grammatically it is.) In spite of the note of discovery in Jethro's exclamation, he is not presented as junior to Moses in knowledge and experience. He is older than Moses and, as we are told in the latter part of the same chapter, he follows his profession of belief in Yahweh by giving Moses practical advice about carrying out his duties as leader. We are told that the next day Jethro found Moses sitting 'to judge the people' and that he was at it 'from the morning unto the evening'. Jethro was astonished that Moses did not know how to delegate responsibility but took care of everything himself. Moses said he had to do it himself, 'because the people come unto me to inquire of God. When they have a matter, they come unto me; and I judge between one and another, and I do make them know the statutes of God, and his laws.' Jethro protested: 'The thing that thou doest is not good. Thou wilt surely wear away, both thou, and this people with thee: for this is too heavy for thee; thou art not able to perform it thyself alone.' And he proceeded to explain how Moses could retain his position as supreme lawgiver while having under him judges – 'able men, such as fear God, men of truth, hating covetousness' – to preside over bodies of different sizes (groups of thousands, hundreds, fifties and tens). Only major matters of principle should be brought to Moses; other matters could be decided by his subordinate judges. 'So Moses hearkened to the voice of his father-in-law, and did all that he said.' And Jethro returned to Midian.

Some scholars have read into the apparent contradictions in this account of the relations between Moses and Jethro (Jethro was Moses' convert, yet Moses was Jethro's pupil) echoes of historical events concerning two different entries into the Promised Land, one by the southern tribes considerably earlier than Moses and a later one by the Joseph tribes (Ephraim and Manasseh) who had been led by Moses out of Egypt. H.H. Rowley has suggested that 'Israelite tribes with Yahweh-worshipping Kenite associates entered Palestine in the Amarna age' (the first half of the fourteenth century BC) about a century before the exodus, and that they perpetuated a more primitive view of Yahweh than the personally rediscovered Yahweh, mediated by Moses, who had adopted Israel as his unique people. The author known as J had the traditions of the former group in mind, while the one known as E had the latter. J would represent the southern tradition, that Yahwism did not begin with Moses, and E would represent the tradition of the northern tribes, to whom Yahweh was mediated by Moses and for whom worship of Yahweh was intimately associated with the deliverance from Egypt and their consecration as Yahweh's unique people. The two traditions were integrated, though we can still find their separate traces. Several versions and modifications of this view have been put forward, and none is more than a hypothesis.

The arrival of Jethro is interposed in the biblical account between the defeat of the Amalekites and the arrival of the children of Israel at Mount Sinai, with the ensuing theophany, the covenant between Yahweh and his people and the revelation of a mass of both ethical and ritual laws. But this does not mean that the 'mount of God' by which Moses was encamped when Jethro came to him is necessarily Sinai. It may well belong to a different tradition altogether, and the description of the children of Israel arriving at Sinai, with which Chapter 19 opens, suggests that this is quite different from the meeting-place of Moses and Jethro. 'In the third month, when the children of Israel were gone forth out of the land of Egypt, the same day came they into the wilderness of Sinai. For . . . they were come to the desert of Sinai, and had pitched in the wilderness; and there Israel camped before the mount.' Moses ascends the mountain, and Yahweh calls to him and makes a pronouncement. The three verses of the pronouncement (19: 4–6) have a rhetorical pattern that suggests a very ancient formulation, which some scholars believe dates back to Moses himself:

Ye have seen what I did unto the Egyptians, and how I bare you on eagles' wings, and brought you unto myself. Now therefore, if ye will obey my voice indeed, and keep my covenant, then ye shall be a peculiar treasure unto me above all people: for all the earth is mine. And ye shall be unto me a kingdom of priests, and a holy nation.

If we omit the section 'Now therefore' to 'keep my covenant', the rhetorical pattern of the original Hebrew is clearer, so these words possibly represent a later interpolation. On the other hand, the pronouncement as it stands sounds as though it might have been the original introduction to the so-called Book of the Covenant given in Exodus 20: 22 to 23: 19. Perhaps we are dealing here with an ancient framework within which a variety of laws were fitted at different times. On this view, the sentences quoted above would be the opening bracket, as it were, and the closing bracket would be Exodus 23: 20–33:

Behold, I send an Angel before thee, to keep thee in the way, and to bring thee into the place which I have prepared. Beware of him, and obey his voice . . . and do all that I speak; then I will be an enemy unto thine enemies, and an adversary unto thine adversaries. For mine Angel shall go before thee and bring thee in unto the Amorites, and the Hittites, and the Perizzites, and the Canaanites, the Hivites, and the Jebusites; and I will cut them off. Thou shalt not bow down to their gods, nor serve them, nor do after their works: but thou shalt utterly overthrow them, and quite break down their images. And ye shall serve Yahweh your God, and he shall bless thy bread and thy water; and I will take sickness away from the midst of thee. . . .

What comes through strongly in both the passages quoted is Yahweh's special relationship with Israel and the importance of the Israelites' separating themselves totally from the abominable cultic practices of the inhabitants of Palestine. About these practices we shall have something to say later; our immediate objective is to try to get behind the somewhat confusing mixture

Moses giving the law: from Alcuin's Bible.

of material in this central part of Exodus to some glimpse of the historical experience that lay behind it.

After Yahweh's pronouncement in Exodus 19: 4–6, quoted above, we are told that Moses summoned the elders and laid Yahweh's words before them. 'And all the people answered together and said, All that Yahweh hath spoken we will do.' (But Yahweh has not yet issued his laws.) Moses reports this response back to Yahweh, who then says to Moses: 'Lo, I come unto thee in a thick cloud, that the people may hear when I speak with thee, and believe thee for ever.' (But we are not told that this happens.) Yahweh then tells Moses to order the people to sanctify themselves for two days, 'for the third day Yahweh will come down in the sight of all the people upon mount Sinai'.

God gives the tables of the law to Moses: fresco from the nave of the church of St Savin, Vienne.

None of the people must come near the mountain, or touch it, on pain of death. The third day arrives, and then comes the quite remarkable account of the events which accompanies God's announcement of what became known as the Ten Commandments. It communicates an extraordinary sense of wonder and excitement:

And it came to pass on the third day in the morning, that there were thunders and lightnings, and a thick cloud upon the mount, and the voice of the trumpet exceeding loud; so that all the people that was in the camp trembled. And Moses brought forth the people out of the camp to meet with God; and they stood at the nether part of the mount. And mount Sinai was altogether on a smoke, because Yahweh descended upon it in fire: and the smoke thereof ascended as the smoke of a furnace, and the whole mount quaked greatly. And when the voice of the trumpet sounded long, and waxed louder and louder, Moses spake, and God answered him by a voice [Exodus 19: 16–19].

Moses then goes up the mountain (apparently for the second time, for in an earlier verse he is said to have come down from the mountain and sanctified the people) and God gives him a repeated charge against letting the people come near, which seems less relevant here, when the theophany has already taken place. It is something of an anticlimax after the account of the smoke and the fire and the mountain quaking, as the trumpet sounded louder and louder until finally God spoke. We would have expected that God's words – given in the following chapter – would have followed immediately on this impressive picture. Instead we get these repetitious sentences and the information that Yahweh sent Moses down from the mountain to give the warning to the people, but told him to come up again with Aaron; the chapter ends without our being told whether they went up again or not.

It is surely a mistake to attempt to explain in purely naturalistic terms the biblical account of the theophany on Sinai. B.D. Eerdmans sees it as arranged by the Kenites, who are described in Numbers 10: 31 as having been with Israel in the wilderness and given Moses valuable advice. The Kenites, being smiths, could set the theatrical scene for Moses with fire and smoke.

The descent of the god of fire, needed for the authority of Moses, was arranged by the Kenites for a fixed day. On this day no one was allowed to go unto the Mountain. They kindled one or more big fires, causing much smoke. They hammered on metal plates, moved torches in the smoke, and gave the signal to bring the people to the nether part of the Mount by blowing a trumpet (shofar) repeatedly, louder and louder. As Moses spoke, he was answered by sound of gongs. The purpose was to hold the people in awe.

This is ingenious, but traditions do not really develop in this way, and it is probably better to believe with Buber that 'every attempt to penetrate to some factual process which is concealed behind the awe-inspiring picture is quite in vain'. Some association of God's might with such natural phenomena as thunder and lightning, some conviction that Israel's God was also the God of nature and that the giving of commandments and the revelation of power over nature were connected, are factors more likely to have been working in the tradition and to have kindled the imagination of the narrator of the impressive passage quoted above.

And what of the familiar commandments spoken by God in Chapter 20? Do they really derive from Moses? They are repeated in Deuteronomy 5: 9–21, with some variations, and in Deuteronomy 4: 13 they are called *aseret ha-d'varim*, which means 'the ten words or statements' rather than 'the ten commandments', a phrase which never occurs in the biblical narrative. This is of some importance, because it enables us to see the first of them, the proclamation 'I am Yahweh thy God, which have brought thee out of the land of Egypt, out of the house of bondage', as a genuine part of the ten, and indeed the basic one, for the identity of the speaker as Yahweh the deliverer of Israel is what gives him the right to command absolute obedience. The Decalogue (as we may call it, to avoid the confusion between commandments and statements) was part of the covenant between God and Israel which is what Israel's encounter with Yahweh at Sinai is all about. It seems likely that the versions we have in Exodus and Deuteronomy are both expansions of statements considerably shorter in form, beginning with the proclamation of Yahweh as God and going on to prohibit worship of other gods, the making of graven images and the taking of Yahweh's name in vain, to enjoin observance of the sabbath and honouring of parents, and to prohibit murder, adultery, stealing (the Hebrew verb used here, *ganav*, was traditionally interpreted to mean man-stealing, the kidnapping of a free person), bearing false witness and coveting (the Hebrew word *chamad* means both to covet and to take). In their original brief form there is every reason to believe them genuinely Mosaic, corresponding as they do to a pronouncement about man's duty to God and his fellow men in the context of recognition of Yahweh as Israel's recent deliverer from Egypt. The ethical ideas they display have much in common with those of other ancient Near Eastern civilizations. The so-called 'Negative Confession' of the Egyptians (*c.* 1500 BC) has the dead man protest before his judge in the next world that he has not stolen or been

OPPOSITE Jebel Katherina, site of the ancient monastery of St Catherine.

OVERLEAF The crossing of the Red Sea, by Luini.

covetous or murdered or committed adultery, and indeed includes other sins against society not included in the Decalogue. The somewhat later Babylonian *Shurpu* lays even greater stress on the social virtues; but the stress on the uniqueness of Yahweh, the prohibition of not only recognizing other gods but even of worshipping Yahweh in some material form (of an animal, for example, a practice so common in Egypt), and the central place of the sabbath, are special to the Mosaic Decalogue. Injunctions given later in Exodus and the following biblical books show a horrified rejection of a variety of practices, from child sacrifice to necromancy, that were common among the Canaanite peoples. How far all of these injunctions can be attributed to Moses is a separate question from that of the origin of the Decalogue. With respect to the latter, there is no reason to reject the tradition that in its original form it was promulgated by Moses. They are ordinances for welding a community, laying down first the nature of the community's God, then, as Buber has pointed out, dealing with the relationship between members of the community in time (they must rest every seventh day, and the relation between the generations is regulated by the precept to honour parents) and then with that relationship in space, 'the with-one-another of the community in so far as it establishes a norm for the mutual relations between its members'. Or, as Gerhard von Rad has put it, 'in the second part the commandment to honour parents comes first, then follow the commandments which protect life, the marriage, the freedom, the reputation and the possessions of fellow men.' There is no mention of circumcision, which indicates an early date because circumcision came to the foreground only after the settled Israelites came into conflict with the Philistines, one of the few peoples of the ancient Near East who did not practise it. And if we take only the first few words of each statement or commandment we find a memorable, easily transmitted formula capable of survival over a vast period of time.

The Decalogue is followed immediately, in the Exodus account, by a further description of the scene at Sinai, which is not easy to relate in any precise way to previous or later descriptions:

And all the people saw the thunderings, and the lightnings, and the noise of the trumpet, and the mountain smoking: and when the people saw it, they removed, and stood afar off. And they said unto Moses, Speak thou with us, and we will hear: but let not God speak with us, lest we die. And the people stood afar off, and Moses drew near unto the thick darkness where God was.

Scenes from the medieval *Golden Haggadah*: the plague of the first-born (top); the crossing of the Red Sea (bottom).

Doré's interpretation of the giving of the law on Mount Sinai.

And God gives Moses instructions about the building of an altar for sacrifices. We are to hear a great deal about sacrifices later: the sacrificing of domestic animals was a practice common to all Western Asiatic religions from the third millennium BC, and was particularly important in Semitic religion, so much so that Moses could not have omitted instructions about it without losing credibility. Its functions in early religion included placating the deity by bringing him gifts, paying him homage, either as an individual or as a community, solemnizing an important occasion in the life of the community, and achieving some kind of communion with the deity by jointly partaking with him in the sacrificial meal. For the Israelites of Moses' time, to sacrifice an animal was the only way of killing it for food, the taking of a domestic animal's life being a solemn ritual act that could only be done with proper religious ceremony. In Deuteronomy 12:15 we find a later tradition recorded, allowing the slaughtering of domestic animals for secular use, though even then certain regulations are to be observed.

We are now in that part of Exodus known as the Book of the Covenant. ('And he [Moses] took the book of the covenant, and read in the audience of the people: and they said, All that Yahweh hath said we will do, and be obedient' Exodus 24: 7.) This contains a variety of legislation concerning the status and rights of individuals, capital offences, bodily injuries, theft and burglary, seduction, idolatrous customs, ritual prescriptions, the importance of equal justice for all men, and finally a cultic calendar dealing with the sabbatical year, the sabbath and the three annual festivals. The mixture of legal, moral and cultic prescriptions is characteristic not only of other lists of regulations found in the Mosaic books (the so-called 'Holiness Code' of Leviticus 17 and the laws in Deuteronomy 12 and 26) but also of other ancient Near Eastern codes. Many parallels have been found between the Book of the Covenant and earlier collections of cuneiform laws, such as the Sumerian law code promulgated by Lipit-Ishtar of Isin (c. 1870 BC), the Akkadian code from the kingdom of Eshunna (of uncertain date but roughly the same period), and the famous code of Hammurapi of Babylon (early seventeenth century BC), also written in Akkadian. The differences between the Book of the Covenant and these codes are nevertheless striking. For example, although slavery was a recognized institution in ancient Israel as elsewhere in the ancient world, the laws about protecting the status and dignity of the slave are unique. 'If thou buy a Hebrew servant, six years he shall serve; and in the seventh he shall go out free for nothing' (Exodus 21: 2). 'Hebrew' here does not mean 'fellow Israelite', as though this was a special regulation for slaves taken from one's own people. Scholars are agreed that the word is here used to refer to a legal or social status – a slave of Habiru-like status – rather than to membership of a particular people. A man cannot smite his servant with impunity, and if he strikes him (or her) so as to inflict a real physical injury, such as putting out an eye or a tooth, he must let him go free. If an ox gores a man or woman fatally, the ox shall be destroyed (but its flesh must not be eaten, for it is now a religiously taboo creature, having destroyed the image of God): its owner goes unpunished unless the ox was known to be a habitual gorer and the owner, knowing this, has refused to keep it confined. The uncompromising demand for the death penalty where the destruction of human life is concerned is paradoxically part of the recognition of the sacredness of human life. Murder cannot be compounded. (This is made quite explicit in a later passage, Numbers 35: 31.)

Many of the laws in the Book of the Covenant are of the form known as 'casuistic', with the basic formula, common to all ancient Near Eastern law-codes, of 'if . . . then' ('if a man steal an ox . . . he shall restore five oxen for an ox'). This is quite different from the 'apodictic' form of the Decalogue which gives direct commands addressed to the listener in the second person singular. But even the casuistic laws are underpinned, in the Book of the Covenant, by the divine sanction, while the categorical nature of the apodictic Decalogue, with its orders and prohibitions *because Yahweh wills it*, is like nothing else in the ancient codes. The code of Hammurapi, for example, is wholly secular in tone. Many commentators hold that in this categorical tone, referring everything to the divine will, we hear the voice of Moses.

The Book of the Covenant bears clear traces of an ancient origin. The casuistic formula itself is ancient; the vocabulary is old; there is no suggestion of a monarchy, but the background is a society organized tribally with the family as an essential unit; there are no laws about commerce or about class distinctions and professions; there is no suggestion of any central law-enforcing authority, but laws punishing non-ritual offences are addressed to the injured party or his next of kin. We have noted parallels with other ancient Near Eastern codes. A startlingly specific parallel is found between Exodus 21 : 4 (the case of a slave to whom his master has given a wife who has borne him children) and a Nuzi document giving the case of a Habiru slave given a wife by his master; the procedure required of the slave when he wishes to renounce his proffered freedom can also be paralleled in a Nuzi document. All this suggests an early origin, certainly before the establishment of the Israelite monarchy about 1,000 BC. At the same time much of it presupposes a settled agricultural rather than a nomadic way of life. It looks like, in Bright's words, 'a description of normative Israelite judicial procedure in the days of the Judges' (*c.* 1200–1020 BC), when they were settled in Palestine. There must have been some, very selective, borrowing from the laws and customs of people of similar stock absorbed into the Israelite community, but whatever was borrowed was given the sanction of Yahweh's will. Thus a Mosaic core may well have been enlarged after the settlement of the Israelites in the Promised Land. But there is no reason to dispute the Mosaic core. The specific penalties for individual offences mentioned in the Book of the Covenant, which are in sharp contrast to the simple command with no mention of penalties of the Decalogue formula (where the implied penalty is, presumably, simply the wrath of Yahweh) may well be post-Mosaic. Some of the more ancient prescriptions may have been developed by those tribes who, many scholars believe, never went to Egypt at all but remained in Palestine where they were eventually joined by those whom Moses led out of Egypt.

The Book of the Covenant presupposes a covenant: it is between Yahweh and the people of Israel and is negotiated by Moses. The laws attributed to

Moses in the Bible, though not all delivered by him, are all fitted into the Mosaic conception in which obedience to Yahweh constitutes Israel's performance of her side of the covenant. There are interesting political parallels in the history of the ancient Near East. The covenant between God and the tribes of Israel described in Exodus 24 has been compared to suzerainty treaties (between the Great King and his vassals) of the Hittite empire and to the covenant made by Urukagina, prince of Lagash (2400 BC) with his god Ningirsu in connection with his legislative reforms. But the covenant of Exodus is unique; it is between a group of wandering tribes who, by entering into the covenant, become a people, and the God both of nature and of history, who becomes, not their *baal*, their lord and master, for *baal* had connotations of duality and mating and was associated with sexual fertility cults, but their *melech*, their king, reigning absolutely alone, thus eliminating the need of any earthly ruler and requiring only a mediator to interpret the divine king's will. There is no trace of this concept anywhere else in ancient history, and in this sense we can agree with H.H.Rowley's observation that 'the religious achievement of Moses was not something that grew naturally out of his environment or circumstances, and the ideas that he mediated to Israel were not derived from Egypt or from any other people'.

Exodus 24 describes the ritual convenant meal. It is a very ancient narrative:

And he said unto Moses, Come up unto Yahweh, thou, and Aaron, Nadab
and Abihu [*the abrupt and unexplained introduction of these two characters, who*
appear as sons of Aaron in P's relatively late contribution, Leviticus 10: 1, may be
either an addition or a vestigial trace of something more substantial that has fallen
out], *and seventy of the elders of Israel; and worship ye afar off. And Moses alone*
shall come near Yahweh: but they shall not come nigh; neither shall the people
go up with him. And Moses came and told the people all the words of Yahweh,
and all the judgements: and all the people answered with one voice, and said, All
the words which Yahweh hath said will we do. And Moses wrote all the words of
Yahweh, and rose up early in the morning, and builded an altar under the hill,
and twelve pillars, according to the twelve tribes of Israel. And he sent young men
of the children of Israel, which offered burnt offerings, and sacrificed peace offerings
of oxen unto the Lord. And Moses took half the blood and put it in basins; and half
of the blood he sprinkled on the altar. And he took the book of the covenant, and
read in the audience of the people: and they said, All that Yahweh hath said will
we do, and be obedient. And Moses took the blood, and sprinkled it on the people,
and said, Behold the blood of the covenant, which Yahweh hath made with you
concerning all these words.
Then went up Moses, and Aaron, Nadab, and Abihu, and seventy of the elders

of Israel; And they saw the God of Israel: and there was under his feet as it were a
paved work of sapphire stone, and as it were the body of heaven in his clearness.
And upon the nobles of the children of Israel he laid not his hand: also they saw
God, and did eat and drink.

This vision seen by Moses and the elders of an invisible God (who refuses to show himself even to Moses alone) stands out in the biblical story as something strange yet somehow authentic. Buber sees it as a recollection of a real event:

They have presumably wandered through clinging, hanging mist before dawn; and at the very moment they reach their goal, the swaying darkness tears asunder (as I myself happened to witness once) and dissolves except for one cloud already transparent with the hue of the still unrisen sun. The sapphire proximity of the heavens overwhelms the aged shepherds of the Delta, who have never before tasted, who have never been given the slightest idea, of what is shown in the play of early light over the summits of the mountains. And this precisely is perceived by the representatives of the liberated tribes as that which lies under the feet of their enthroned *Melek.*

It would be pleasant to think that some such experience underlies the remarkable biblical account.

And Yahweh said unto Moses, Come up to me into the mount, and be there:
and I will give thee tables of stone, and a law, and commandments which I have
written; that thou mayest teach them. . . . And Moses went up into the mount, and
a cloud covered the mount. And the glory of Yahweh abode upon mount Sinai, and
the cloud covered it six days: and the seventh day he called unto Moses out of the
midst of the cloud. And the sight of the glory of Yahweh was like devouring fire
on the top of the mount in the eyes of the children of Israel. And Moses went into
the midst of the cloud, and gat him up into the mount: and Moses was in the
mount forty days and forty nights.

For all the clarity of the vision of the sapphire heavens, the account of Moses' ascents of Sinai is blurred. It is impossible to make out exactly how many times he went up and down (even one ascent and descent would be quite a feat for a man of eighty, as we are told he then was!) and precisely what happened when. But it is clear that we have in this chapter a very ancient tradition about the making of the covenant. It is something of an anticlimax, and to the modern reader a disappointment, when this is immediately followed by an account in the most minute detail of the instructions Yahweh gives Moses on the mountain for the making of the portable tent sanctuary and all the apparatus required for cultic worship. This is clearly a later insertion by P, with his emphasis on the priestly and the cultic. The writer does not pause to inquire where, in the wilderness, the Israelites would be able to get the gold, silver, brass, fine linen, porpoise-skins, onyx stones, and other precious material required for this extraordinary structure and its equipment. Much later material, some of it relating to the Temple, has entered into this account, which does not mean that the Israelites did not have a tent sanctuary with them in their wanderings. The account of the ark (the tabernacle being essentially the edifice to contain the ark) is clearly old. This chest of acacia wood overlaid with pure gold is to be the depository of the stone tablets Moses brings down from Sinai but, more significantly, it – or rather its top part or cover, *kapporet*, flanked by two cherubim – is a symbolic throne or footstool for Yahweh; 'and there', he tells Moses, 'I will meet with thee and commune with thee . . . from between the two cherubim.' Yahweh having been recognized by covenant as Israel's king, 'the Royal Covenant', as Buber has put it, 'is followed by the building of the Throne.' But all this is an interruption of the story of Moses on Sinai, which should move directly from Exodus 24: 18, where we see Moses disappearing up the mountain to commune with God for forty days and forty nights, to Exodus 31: 18: 'And he gave unto Moses, when he had made an end of communing with him upon mount Sinai, two tables of testimony, tables of stone, written with the finger of God.' It is generally assumed that what was written on the tablets was the Decalogue, though this is not stated.

6

Difficulties of a Chosen People

The story of Moses' secluding himself on the mountain top for forty days and forty nights brings in again the theme of solitary meditation and discovery that we found in the story of the burning bush. Forty is of course a symbolic figure, found frequently in the Bible in connection with a significant period of time, and a forty-day disappearance on a cloud-enwrapped mountain suggests the relationship between loneliness and revelation that is central in the Moses tradition. But the account in Chapter 32 of Exodus of the people growing resentful at Moses' absence and demanding a visible image of the deity that was supposed to be leading them shows the gap between Moses' intermittent need for isolated self-communion on the one hand and the requisites of successful popular leadership on the other. For we must remember the novelty and strangeness of the conception of God mediated by Moses. Yahweh had adopted Israel as his special people, he had led them out of Egypt and delivered them at the Reed Sea, and he had entered into a covenant with them which offered protection on his part and demanded obedience to his commands on the people's part. Yet the only real sign of his presence was the ark, assuming it to have been built by this time, a portable footstool for an invisible God; none of the paraphernalia and panoply of images and visual

Aaron and the golden candlestick, by Chagall.

128

ABOVE The bull Apis, worshipped by the Egyptians. BELOW An Assyrian cylinder seal showing bull worship, 11th century BC.

symbols which vividly proclaimed the presence of other nations' gods were allowed by Moses, for Yahweh was different and unique. The story of the people's demanding the kind of image that was so regularly associated with other nations' worship is evidence of the novelty of the concept of the divine presented to them by Moses. The God of nature, of history and of the moral order dwelling invisibly on high and making the most exacting demands on the people he adopted as peculiarly his own – there is nothing like this in the traditions of any other ancient people. However primitive we may consider the early Israelites' conception of Yahweh to have been, however much later ideas may have subtilized and sophisticated the original Mosaic ideas into an advanced ethical monotheism, there can be no doubt of the great gap between the Mosaic concept of the deity and commonly held ideas on the same subject at the time of the exodus. We have mentioned earlier Moses' habit of putting new wine into old bottles, of using traditional forms and practices while introducing startling novelties: but though this could in some respects make the novelties acceptable by having them viewed in a more or less familiar context (of cultic practices, for example), there were bound to be occasions when a sense of the strangeness and the *difference* of Yahweh's worship overcame the people, and they wanted to be allowed to behave more like other people. So when Moses' physical presence was removed for a considerable period of time, 'the people gathered themselves together unto Aaron, and said unto him, Up, make us gods, which shall go before us; for as for this Moses, the man that brought us up out of the land of Egypt, we wot not what is become of him.' And Aaron collected the people's gold earrings and made them a golden calf, which they hailed, saying 'These be thy gods (*elohim*) O Israel which brought thee out of the land of Egypt.'

This story is clearly related to the account in I Kings 27–8 of King Jeroboam making two calves of gold and saying to the people, 'It is too much for you to go up to Jerusalem: behold thy gods, O Israel, which brought thee up out of the land of Egypt.' This shows that a tradition that God could be worshipped in the form of a calf (or small bull) was known in Israel in the latter part of the tenth century BC and that it was associated with the story of the defection before Mount Sinai. But the Exodus story must be older than that in Kings (rather than, as some scholars have argued, a later insertion in the light of the Jeroboam story) because of the declaration about being brought out of Egypt, which makes immediate sense in the context of Exodus but seems an irrelevant historical echo in Kings. It is important to realize that in neither case are the people described as forsaking Yahweh, but rather as worshipping him

OVERLEAF *The Adoration of the Golden Calf*, by Poussin.

(though in a plural form) by regarding a bull as the seat of the invisible God. The early Semitic god Hadan – god of mountain and storm and, by extension, of fertility – was represented on Syrian reliefs as standing on a bull; his cult was widespread in Canaan. The bull was the god's seat, not an image of the god himself. When Aaron gave in to the people's demands, he did not regard himself as forsaking Yahweh. When he saw the people hailing the golden calf, 'he built an altar before it; and Aaron made proclamation, and said, Tomorrow is a feast to Yahweh.' In other words, Aaron is represented as giving in to the people's demand for a symbolic visual representation of Yahweh. It was not the command to 'have no other gods before me' that proved too difficult; it was the next commandment, that 'thou shalt not make unto thee a graven image'. Perhaps it was too much to ask. Certainly Christianity was to relax this commandment from an early period, and the history of the place of images in Roman Catholic worship suggests that Moses was trying to eradicate a deep-seated human impulse.

Why Aaron is shown as having played such a prominent part in the golden calf episode is not clear. It has been suggested by those who believe that the primary golden calf story is the one concerning Jeroboam in I Kings that worship of Yahweh by means of a bull image in the time of the monarchy was believed to have been originally sanctioned by Aaron, and that the Exodus story is a deliberate attempt to discredit Aaron in order to stamp out the use of the bull. But this seems a rather extravagant hypothesis. What emerges in the text of Exodus as we have it is the difference between Moses, meek yet stern and absolute in his ethical and ritual demands, and the compromising character of Aaron, who did not share Moses' lonely visions and did not possess his brother's absolute sense of mission. The historical reality behind the stories of Aaron remains shadowy, but in the golden calf episode the real emphasis is on the character of Moses and of the God whose character and demands he mediates to the people. Moses is revealed as the non-compromiser, as opposed to Aaron, but also, and perhaps more significantly, as intercessor. Yahweh tells Moses on the mountain that his (Moses') people have turned to worshipping and sacrificing to a golden calf (Yahweh will not accept that the calf can be in any way a symbol of himself). They are, says Yahweh, 'a stiffnecked people':

Now therefore let me alone, that my wrath may wax hot against them, and that I may consume them: and I will make of thee a great nation. And Moses besought Yahweh his God, and said, Yahweh, why doth thy wrath wax hot against thy people, which thou hast brought forth out of the land of Egypt with great power, and with a mighty hand? Wherefore should the Egyptians speak, and say, For mischief did he bring them out, to slay them in the mountains, and to consume them from the face of the earth? Turn from thy fierce wrath, and repent of this evil against thy people. Remember Abraham, Isaac, and Israel, thy servants, to whom thou swarest by thine own self, and saidst unto them, I will multiply your seed as the stars of heaven, and all this land that I have spoken of will I give unto your seed, and they shall inherit it for ever. And Yahweh repented of the evil which he thought to do unto his people [Exodus 32: 10–14].

So Moses turns to descend the mountain, with the two engraved tables of stone in his hand. 'The tables were written on both their sides; on the one side and the other were they written.' This is an interesting detail, indicating the extraordinary nature of the tables; we know of no ancient stones engraved on both sides: stelae were inscribed on one side only. These two tables of stone were the actual physical embodiment of the covenant between Yahweh and Israel. 'And the tables were the work of God, and the writing was the writing of God, graven upon the tables.' As Moses comes further down the mountain (now, we are suddenly told, accompanied by Joshua), the sound of revelry comes up from below. The dialogue between Moses and Joshua that ensues, as Buber has pointed out, bears all the marks of being vestiges of a primitive ballad. A literal translation from the Hebrew will bring this out:

> Joshua: Noise of war in the camp.
> Moses: Not the noise of the cry of warriors
> And not the noise of the cry of defeat
> But the noise of revelry I hear.

('Of revelry' is conjectural. Something has clearly dropped out of the Hebrew text, where the last line reads 'but noise I hear'. Buber conjectures 'a word with the meaning of riot' and assumes that 'there must certainly have been a riot'.) When Moses had descended far enough to see the people dancing round the golden calf, his 'anger waxed hot, and he cast the tables out of his hands, and brake them beneath the mount'. The breaking of the tables signified, according to the standard practice of the ancient Near East, the breaking of the covenant. The people having broken their side of the agreement, it is now null and void and in order to indicate this its physical embodiment is destroyed. If Yahweh, persuaded by the intercession of Moses to forgive the people, wishes to reassume them as his special people, he will have to write a new covenant, which in fact is what he is to do.

What had begun as a desire for a visual representation of their God had developed into an orgy. We are told in Exodus 32: 25 that the people were dancing naked. The tradition here seems to be that the serving of God by means of an image is the thin end of a wedge: the thick end is every kind of orgiastic licence and 'abomination' which the Mosaic code is dedicated to stamping out. With this sort of thing there can be no compromise whatever. The Mosaic code is divinely ordained and absolute, to be scrupulously observed with dedicated obedience. Any lapse is both disloyalty to Yahweh and destructive of the community. This notion runs so fiercely through the Mosaic books of the Bible that it is reasonable to attribute it to Moses himself. An uncompromising code, forged in the wilderness away from the soft corruption of cities, a code proclaimed from a mountain in the desert to a group of wandering tribes living in spartan conditions, it is an appropriate code for a people who are eventually to be led into the Promised Land and there extirpate all those who worship false gods, practise fertility cults, ritual prostitution, child sacrifice and other abominations. We must bear this in mind when we read in Exodus 32: 20–7 of Moses' savage reaction to what he found. He may have pleaded with Yahweh to forgive his people, but he himself knew what had to be done if there were to remain a people worthy of forgiveness: those who persisted in evil doing, who would not proclaim themselves as on Yahweh's side, had to be stamped out. There is no claim now that what went on around the golden calf was a form of worship of Yahweh, which is how it all began: it is apostasy to Yahweh. So, having burnt the calf, ground it into powder, and made the people drink it, Moses proclaimed: 'Who is on Yahweh's side? let him come unto me.' The sons of Levi gathered at the call, to rally to Moses. (This looks very like a later historical justification of the monopolistic role of the Levites in public worship.) But there is some ambiguity in the account, for, although 'all the sons of Levi' rallied to Yahweh, Moses ordered them to 'slay every man his brother'. It is a terrible command: 'Thus saith Yahweh God of Israel, Put every man his sword by his side, and go in and out from gate to gate throughout the camp, and slay every man his brother, and every man his companion, and every man his neighbour.' So there seems to have been an internecine struggle among the Levites themselves. About three thousand men were killed, we are told, and after this slaughter Moses told the people to consecrate themselves anew to Yahweh that he might bestow a blessing upon them. There is also a perfunctory reference to a plague which the Lord sent on the people as punishment. But Moses returned to Yahweh 'and said, Oh, this people have sinned a great sin, and have made them gods of gold. Yet now, if thou wilt forgive their sin – ; and if not, blot me, I pray thee, out of thy book which thou hast written.' No, replies Yahweh, I will blot out only those who have sinned. But the people as a whole are spared. 'Therefore now go, lead the people unto the place of which I have spoken unto thee: behold, mine Angel shall go before thee.' He renews his promise to give to their descendants the land promised to the Patriarchs,

Moses breaking the tables of the law, by Doré.

but he will no longer accompany them on their journeyings; 'for thou art a stiffnecked people; lest I consume thee by the way.'

The note turns from the denunciatory to the elegiac. There is a strange, isolated passage in Exodus 33, evidently of great antiquity, describing how Moses no longer felt able to pitch his tent in the midst of the camp, where the people could be all around him, but he 'pitched it without the camp, afar off from the camp, and called it the Tabernacle of the congregation. . . . And it

137

came to pass, when Moses went out unto the tabernacle, that all the people rose, and stood every man at his tent door, and looked after Moses, until he was gone into the tabernacle.' This tent or tabernacle of Moses is not the same as the tabernacle or 'tent of meeting', the sanctuary that Yahweh had already instructed Moses how to make. This was his own private tent, now pitched outside the camp that had been polluted by image-worship and debauchery. 'And it came to pass, as Moses entered into the tabernacle, the cloudy pillar descended, and stood at the door of the tabernacle, and Yahweh talked with Moses. And all the people saw the cloudy pillar stand at the tabernacle door: and all the people rose up and worshipped, every man in his tent door.' The Hebrew verbs in this passage are all in the imperfect: this is how it used to be, this is the procedure that developed. It could best be rendered in English as '. . . all the people would rise and stand every man at his tent door . . . and as Moses entered into the tabernacle, the cloudy pillar would descend. . . .' The picture accentuates the loneliness of Moses. The people watch in wonder and awe as he communes with God alone in his tent outside the camp: he is now further away from them and nearer to the divine.

What emerges from the account in Exodus at this point is the price Moses has to pay for mediating between the divine and the human. He loses some of his ordinary human contacts as he becomes more engrossed in the divine. In Exodus 33: 12–16 he asks Yahweh for further reassurance that he really still considers Israel his people, especially since Yahweh has said he will no longer be with the people in their journeyings. Yahweh replies, 'My presence shall go with thee, and I will give thee rest.' But Moses wants further reassurance, some kind of special personal vision that will confirm his sense of God's presence. It is a strange passage:

And Yahweh said unto Moses, I will do this thing also that thou hast spoken: for thou hast found grace in my sight, and I know thee by name. And he said, I beseech thee, show me thy glory. And he said, I will make all my goodness pass before thee, and I will proclaim the name of Yahweh before thee; and I will be gracious to whom I will be gracious, and will show mercy on whom I will show mercy. And he said, thou canst not see my face: for there shall no man see me, and live. And Yahweh said, Behold, there is a place by me, and thou shalt stand upon a rock. And it shall come to pass, while my glory passeth by, that I will put thee in a cleft of the rock, and will cover thee with my hand while I pass by. And I will take away my hand, and thou shalt see my back parts; but my face shall not be seen [Exodus 33: 17–24].

Moses breaks the tables of the law – Chagall's version.

139

But first Moses had to hew two new tables of stone, on which Yahweh would again write 'the words which were on the first tables'. Then Yahweh passed by him and proclaimed his own qualities: 'Yahweh, Yahweh, God merciful and gracious, long-suffering and abundant in goodness and truth, keeping mercy for thousands, forgiving iniquity and transgression and sin, and that will by no means clear the guilty; visiting the iniquity of the fathers upon the children, and upon the children's children, unto the third and to the fourth generation.' Mercy and forgiveness are emphasized first, then without pause we have mention of punishment of the guilty unto the third and fourth generation. Forgiveness presumably depends on repentance and reformation, while stubbornness in evil-doing will not be forgiven. There is a dialectic at work here, which is not fully worked out. Immediately after this follows Yahweh's explicit renewal of the covenant and the giving of another set of commandments, the so-called 'ritual decalogue' or cultic commandments. When Moses returned with the two new tables after this further communion with Yahweh (once again for forty days and forty nights) the children of Israel found that they could not look directly on his face, for 'the skin of his face shone' so that he had to wear a veil when talking with the people. This is a fascinating symbol of the consequences of Moses' increasing communion with the divine: his lonely mystic visions, while not impairing his leadership, were increasingly setting him apart from the people.

There has been a great deal of scholarly debate about the significance of the 'ritual decalogue' in Exodus 34: 12–27. It is introduced by Yahweh saying to Moses: 'Behold, I make a covenant,' and promising to drive out the inhabitants of Canaan before the advancing Israelites if they obey Yahweh's commands. The first of the commands that follow prohibits making a covenant with these inhabitants and enjoins the destruction of their altars, images and sacred places. They must worship only Yahweh and make no molten images. They must keep the feast of unleavened bread, offer the firstborn of their sheep and cattle, rest on the seventh day (even 'in earing time and in harvest'), observe 'the feast of weeks, of the firstfruits of wheat harvest, and the feast of ingathering at the year's end'. These are two harvest festivals, and together with the feast of unleavened bread they constitute the three festivals on which Moses is then told all Israelite males must appear before Yahweh. The commandments conclude: 'Thou shalt not offer the blood of my sacrifice with leaven; neither shall the sacrifice of the feast of the passover be left unto the morning. The first of the firstfruits of thy land thou shalt bring unto the house of Yahweh thy God. Thou shalt not seethe a kid in its mother's milk.'

The first things that strike us about these commandments – which in fact are twelve or perhaps thirteen in number, although it is often assumed that they were originally ten, hence the term 'ritual *decalogue*' – is that they deal with ritual and not ethical matters and that they take for granted a people leading a settled agricultural life. Earlier scholars, who somewhat naively assumed that cultic and ritual ordinances always preceded ethical ones, took these to be the original ten commandments, and supported their view by drawing attention to the fact that immediately after they are presented we are told that Yahweh 'wrote upon the tables the words of the covenant, the ten commandments' (*d'varim*, words). But we now know that the simple evolutionary view that civilization advances from the cultic to the ethical is quite untenable. We have abundant anthropological evidence that cultic or ritual rules develop side by side with ethical imperatives and may well go on developing long after the basic ethical pattern has been set. Further, the fact that these commandments assume a settled agricultural life in Palestine suggest that, at least in part, they date from after the settlement of the people of Israel in Palestine. Some of them echo and some of them supplement commands in the Book of the Covenant (Exodus 20: 22 to 23: 19), which again suggests that they are later than the well known Decalogue of Chapter 20. Perhaps, it has been conjectured, they derive from the house-book of a Palestinian sanctuary prepared from old material after the settlement in Palestine. Elements in both sets of injunctions must go back to pre-Mosaic times. The hand of Moses seems clearly visible in Exodus 20; how far it is also to be discerned in Chapter 34 is difficult to determine. The 'ritual decalogue' may represent a post-settlement adaptation of a pre-Mosaic code with only minimal Mosaic influence.

The modern mind finds it difficult to look sympathetically at the habit of mind which puts the ritual and the ethical on the same level of significance. But this habit is common to all the ancient Near Eastern religions (to go no further afield) and the setting side by side of profound moral commandments and what may appear to us meaningless ritual observances is by no means unique to ancient Israel. The juxtaposition even of ritual commands may seem inexplicable to us, as in the conclusion of the passage under discussion: 'The firstfruits of thy land thou shalt bring unto the house of Yahweh thy God. Thou shalt not seethe a kid in its mother's milk.' Bringing firstfruits to God may be seen as an offering of thanksgiving, and what this has to do with refraining from boiling a kid in its mother's milk is not evident. No reasons are ever given for such ritual laws. It is Yahweh's will, and that is that. In fact, however, we know from the Ras Shamra tablets that boiling a kid in its mother's milk was a practice of Canaanite religion, so this seems to be another of those *differentiating* laws which figure so prominently in the code given to Israel, a people described as a 'peculiar treasure' (Exodus 19: 5). The Hebrew word

The wilderness of Sinai.

translated as 'peculiar treasure' is *segullah*, which means a treasured possession and by extension a privileged person: a recently discovered Ugaritic text shows the word used in the sense of an especially privileged vassal. The association of privilege with special duties pervades the Mosaic code. The people of Israel must be different, 'a kingdom of priests and a holy nation' (Exodus 19: 6), and the function of many of the ritual laws seems to have been to emphasize this. At the same time there is genuine moral horror at the rites of

the Canaanite peoples, especially their association of certain sexual practices with divine worship. The penetration of Canaanite practices into Israel after their settlement in the Promised Land led to the regular revival and elaboration of denunciations of such practices, but there is no reason to doubt that Moses himself made the deliberate decision to separate his people in a striking way from the religious practices of both Egyptians and Canaanites. So while the religious code presented in different places in the Mosaic books of the Bible reflects in many ways the habits of mind and the ritual practices of the

whole Near Eastern ancient world (in its attitude to sacrifices, priestly cere-
monial, certain purification rites, etc.) it is at the same time a protest against
those habits and practices. Once again we see the combination of the traditional and the innovative that is so characteristic of the Mosaic tradition.

There remains the problem of what exactly we are to understand was
carved on the second set of tables. Presumably it was the original Decalogue
that was on the first tables. Yet immediately after the presentation of the
'cultic decalogue' we are told (Exodus 34: 28) that Moses 'wrote upon the
tables the words of the covenant, the ten words'. This suggests that the ten
'words' refer to the immediately preceding ritual commandments rather
than to the original ethical Decalogue that was on the first tables. What has
apparently happened here is that two different traditions of the terms of the
covenant have been put together. The original writer of Exodus 34: 28 may
well have meant the 'ten words' to refer to the ethical Decalogue but the
redactor who included it at this point surely thought of it as referring to what
immediately precedes it in the same chapter. We are dealing here with variations in the traditions about Moses and the covenant at Sinai that developed
after Moses' own time. It is in fact impossible to derive a wholly coherent
picture of what occurred from the biblical account. To take only two
examples: Moses' vision of the back of Yahweh takes place on the mountain,
yet immediately afterwards Moses is summoned to the mountain and told to
ascend it; and in Exodus 34: 28 we are specifically told that it was Moses who
wrote the words on the second set of tables, which flatly contradicts the first
verse of the same chapter, where Yahweh himself says he will write them.

The remainder of Exodus is taken up with a detailed account of the building
of the tabernacle and the making of the priestly garments, instructions about
which had already been given. The work is finally completed:

Then a cloud covered the tent of the congregation, and the glory of Yahweh
filled the tabernacle. And Moses was not able to enter into the tent of the
congregation, because the cloud abode thereon, and the glory of Yahweh filled
the tabernacle. And when the cloud was taken up from over the tabernacle, the
children of Israel went onward in all their journeys. But if the cloud were not
taken up, then they journeyed not till the day that it was taken up. For the cloud of
Yahweh was upon the tabernacle by day, and fire was on it by night, in the sight
of all the house of Israel, throughout all their journeys.

God's threat not to accompany the people on their journeyings is apparently

OPPOSITE Moses receiving the tables of the law, from the mosaics at San Vitale in Ravenna.
OVERLEAF The fall of manna, by Poussin.

MOSE

forgotten, for this is a strong statement of the actuality of the divine presence. The point of this passage is that though the people depart from the mountain of Yahweh, Yahweh is not left behind. Throughout their stay at Sinai the divine presence, symbolized by the cloud and the fire, had rested on top of the mountain: now it went forth with the people and by its manifestations directed them when to travel and when to stop. The point is made more specifically in Numbers 9: 17: 'And when the cloud was taken up from the tabernacle, then after that the children of Israel journeyed: and in the place where the cloud abode, there the children of Israel pitched their tents.' The tradition of divine guidance through the wilderness and eventually into the Promised Land – a tradition inextricably associated with the leadership of Moses – is emphatically reaffirmed. This leads straight into Leviticus, where Yahweh calls to Moses out of the tabernacle and gives him further instructions.

Leviticus is the work of the priestly writer and is relevant to a study of Moses only in that the vast amount of ritual prescriptions in this book were assimilated into the Mosaic tradition and thus attributed to Moses. And though no objective modern scholar would hold that Moses wrote all the laws attributed to him in the Mosaic books of the Bible, most of them would agree that, in John Bright's words, 'he laid down the constitutive stipulations of covenant to which all specific laws must conform, and whose intent it must seek to express'. The laws given in Leviticus are ethical as well as ritual, although the latter are more numerous. There is a detailed account of methods and categories of sacrifice; an account of the inaugural service of the tabernacle (conducted by Moses) and the ritual installation of Aaron and his sons as priests; laws concerning impurities, which include categories of allowed and forbidden animal food and laws about pollution, infection, contagious diseases and ritual impurities. Chapters 17 to 26, which include the so-called 'Holiness Code', contain an interesting mixture of ritual and ethical injunctions, including the statement that whoever slaughters an animal for food in a purely secular context outside the sanctuary is guilty of murder, a view which, as we have seen, is expressly denied in Deuteronomy, which permits secular slaughter of animals for food. Laws against incest, sodomy and bestiality, against the sacrificing of children in fire to Moloch and against worshipping idols and molten gods are set side by side with laws about leaving gleanings for the poor during the harvest, laws against stealing, defrauding, tale-bearing, corrupt judging and the taking of vengeance, the famous injunction 'thou shalt love thy neighbour as thyself', laws against the miscegenation of cattle and the wearing of garments 'mingled of linen and woollen', against eating

Moses on Mount Sinai (top), and the worship of the Golden Calf (bottom): from the late 13th-century manuscript *La Somme le Ray*, illuminated by Honoré.

anything with blood, shaving the corners of the beard and cutting one's flesh as a sign of mourning, the command to be kind to the stranger and 'love him as thyself' ('for ye were strangers in the land of Egypt') and regulations about just weights and measures. Also forbidden are the practice of magic, the cursing of parents, adultery with another man's wife, and various abominable practices of other nations. 'And ye shall not walk in the manners of the nation, which I cast out before you: for they committed all these things, and therefore I abhorred them. . . . And ye shall be holy unto me: for I Yahweh am holy, and have severed you from other people, that ye should be mine.' Chapter 21 contains a repetition of the commands against any kind of self-mutilation as a sign of mourning (a common custom among the surrounding people) and prescribes the savage penalty of burning for the priest's daughter who profanes herself by playing the whore. (The drive against sacred prostitution and other sexual activities associated with Canaanite fertility rites was especially fierce.) There follow rules about priests and about the observance of the sabbath and the three annual festivals, and a further collection of mixed ethical and ritual laws. Leviticus concludes: 'These are the commandments which Yahweh commanded Moses for the children of Israel in mount Sinai.'

Can we come to any conclusions about the part played by Moses in the promulgation of the laws given in Exodus and Leviticus, apart from the generalizations that have been made above? There is no agreement among scholars, but a common legal core has been traced in all the commandments attributed to Moses and it is reasonable to associate this core with Moses' achievement in instituting a reform in both the cultic and the ethical practices of his people. On the cultic side, there are the repeated insistence on the sabbath, the passover and the other festivals, the offering of firstlings (of both animals and crops), the destruction of idols and the prohibition of Canaanite practices, especially sorcery and witchcraft; and on the ethical side there are the periodical liberation of slaves, the year of release, the law of punishment in kind or *lex talionis* ('an eye for an eye and a tooth for a tooth' – designed to replace the practice of revenge and ensuing endless feuding by a limited and precisely equivalent judicial penalty that would 'make the punishment fit the crime' regardless of the social status of the criminal), impartial justice in the courts and special consideration for the resident alien and the poor. These are found in all the codes presented at intervals throughout the different Mosaic books and may reasonably be taken as lying at the heart of the Mosaic tradition and thus promulgated by Moses himself.

So perhaps we may put these minimal laws beside the more general characteristics we have already noted as central to the Mosaic tradition and therefore likely to derive from the historical Moses. There is another point, that is more conjectural but in a way more interesting. The alternation in Moses' behaviour between mingling with the people and withdrawing from them, the changes in his reports of Yahweh's attitude from stern denunciation to forgiveness, the contrast between Moses' moving plea to Yahweh to forgive the people and his ruthless punishment of them after he has descended the mount and found them dancing round the golden calf – does not all this suggest some deep inner tension deriving perhaps from a fundamental duality in Moses' conception of himself as the father of his people? Amateur psychoanalysis of the dead is dangerous, and it is even more dangerous when the person discussed is only dimly perceived through the mists of tradition. But it is hard to resist the belief that we are dealing here with the kind of struggle between love and the belief in salutary punishment that is common enough among fathers, especially of earlier generations. Moses belongs to his people (what else does the story of his intervening in favour of the Hebrew slave mean?) and at the same time he distances himself from them, for he has to preserve his special function and his authority. He suffers for them and intercedes for them, yet he is capable of punishing them pitilessly. The contradictions in Moses' own behaviour as reported in the Bible may even be related to the duality in the code associated with his name, a code which presents a long-suffering and merciful God who has selected the people of Israel for special love and favour and who nevertheless (or perhaps *therefore*) punishes them with great harshness whenever they are guilty of backsliding. The election of Israel meant both special privileges and special duties. Perhaps it was essentially a Mosaic point that the prophet Amos was later to make when he declared in the name of the Lord: 'You only have I known of all the families of the earth: therefore I will punish you for all your iniquities.'

7

Achievement and Frustration

We have no clear biblical account of what happened between the revelation at Sinai and the entry into the Promised Land. The Book of Numbers, which follows Leviticus, does indeed tell of events from the departure from Sinai to the first stage of the conquest of Canaan and the establishment of the children of Israel east of the River Jordan ready to cross over and enter the land to the west. But the account is presented in such a confused mass of material from different sources (including other parts of the Old Testament) that neither a chronological story nor a clear itinerary can be certainly traced. Nevertheless there are early and genuine traditions preserved in Numbers that throw some light on the activities of Moses during the years of journeying in the wilderness and also on his relations with his people.

Numbers begins with an account of the numbering and listing of able-bodied men capable of bearing arms and of other preparations, many of them purely cultic, for further journeying. The numbers are meticulously broken down by tribes, and the total number of over six hundred thousand agrees with the number given in Exodus 38:26, on whose unrealistic and anachronistic nature we have already commented. But though the figures are unbelievable, some on the names in the list seem to be genuinely ancient – none is formed with 'Ya-' as was later the practice in Israel – and it looks as though an old traditional list has found its way into the narrative. Further evidence of the antiquity of this list has been found in the presence of names with elements such as 'zur' and 'ammi' which are known from recently excavated tables in old Akkadian to have been in use in the ancient city of Mari, on the middle Euphrates, which dominated Mesopotamia in the second half of the eighteenth century BC: according to Martin Noth, such names were 'current in a stratum of population which had many relationships with ancient Israel'. Mari tablets also show a census used both for military purposes and for the assignment of land. So there may be pre-Mosaic elements in the list. It is likely that Moses played a dominant part in organizing the people after leading them out of Egypt, and it is eminently reasonable to suppose that the tradition preserved here of his numbering them by clans and families for the purpose of finding out their true military potential is a genuine echo of his having done so, even though later material has become absorbed into the biblical account. The material about the organization of the Levites and their special duties is more dubiously associated with Moses. The injunction in Numbers 3: 9–10 that the Levites are to be wholly at the disposal of Aaron and his sons, the priests, to wait on them and serve them, looks like a deliberate attempt, made long after the time of Moses, to disparage the status of the Levites vis-à-vis the priests, the descendants of Aaron.

The cultic ordinances of Numbers 5 and 6, including detailed laws about the treatment of ritual uncleanness, may represent partly later practice attributed to Mosaic legislation and partly pre-Mosaic practices tolerated, accepted or endorsed by Moses. The extraordinary details of the trial by ordeal that must be undergone by a woman whom, in a fit of jealousy, her husband has accused of having associated with another man (she must drink 'bitter water' made from dust taken from the floor of the tabernacle, and if she is guilty her bowels and belly will swell and her thigh rot) are startlingly primitive, and though the name of Yahweh and a reference to the tabernacle have been introduced to assimilate the passage to Mosaic legislation, it is so unlike anything else attributed to Moses that is is tempting to regard it as a pre-Mosaic survival.

At the end of a number of cultic laws, all said to be delivered by Yahweh through Moses, we are told that Yahweh commanded Moses to speak to Aaron and his sons and gave them the formula for blessing the people. This simple and eloquent formula may well be Mosaic ('Yahweh' is here translated 'the Lord' as in the Authorized Version, for the passage is so familiar in this form.)

The Lord bless thee, and keep thee:
The Lord make his face shine upon thee and be gracious unto thee:
The Lord lift up his countenance upon thee, and give thee peace.
[Numbers 6: 24–6].

It is interesting that, although this is a formula for blessing 'the children of Israel', the recipient of the blessing is repeatedly addressed in the second person singular, which seems to give it more immediacy (in the Hebrew certainly, for it reminds us of the second person singular of the Ten Commandments) and to ensure, as with the Commandments, that it is received personally by each member of the community. In the threefold repetition of 'Yahweh' ('the Lord') the identity of the author of the blessing is emphasized. The blessing invokes God's protection and his gifts of happiness, prosperity and harmonious fulfilment. (The Hebrew word *shalom*, with which the blessing concludes, does mean peace, as the Authorized Version translates it, but it derives from a root suggesting 'completeness', 'wholeness' or 'harmonious well-being', and this sense is present together with the meaning of 'peace' in the Hebrew wording of the blessing.) It should be noted that it is a blessing for this life. Like all the Mosaic ordinances, it knows nothing of rewards and punishments in an afterlife. The purpose of the Mosaic legislation was to enable individuals and the community to lead full and prosperous lives under the protection of Yahweh: the rewards promised for obedience to Yahweh were peace and prosperity in a land flowing with milk and honey, and the consequences of disobedience were defined in similar earthly terms, starvation, disease and defeat in war. From the moment when Moses first intervened to rescue a fellow Hebrew from a brutal overseer, the biblical narrative makes it clear that his main interest was the condition of the people. He discovered and encountered God in loneliness, but the God he discovered was essentially a protecting lawgiver who enunciated commands to the people in their own interests – not in the interests of their eternal salvation, for such a concept was quite foreign to Moses' way of thinking, but in the interests of their earthly welfare. True, Yahweh was a 'jealous God', and this concept of a God who insisted on being worshipped alone as the God of nature and history and the source of both cultic and ethical imperatives does seem to be genuinely Mosaic; but this did not alter the objectives that Moses, always speaking in the name of that God, proclaimed for his people.

It is not until we come to Numbers 9: 15 that the narrative thread that led from the liberation from Egypt to the events at Sinai is taken up again. Here

Kadesh-barnea, the oasis which became the Israelites' base.

we encounter, for the first time since Chapter 34 of Exodus, the sources that embody the oldest traditions about Moses and the events in the wilderness. We are told of the function of the pillar of cloud by day and of fire by night in guiding the Israelites in their journeyings and in indicating where and for how long they should stop; and in Chapter 10 we are told of the departure from Sinai and the ordering of the people both for marching and for warfare. 'And it came to pass on the twentieth day of the second month, in the second year, that the cloud was taken from off the tabernacle of the testimony. And the children of Israel took their journeys out of the wilderness of Sinai; and the cloud rested on the wilderness of Paran.' We cannot certainly identify the wilderness of Paran, but if we accept the view that Mount Sinai is Jebel Katherina then their route lay to the north (after an initial movement north-westward) and Paran must lie north of Mount Sinai and considerably south of Kadesh-barnea, which they eventually reached and which became their most important base. Noth connects the name Paran 'with that of the *wādi ferān* in the mountainous southern part of the Sinai peninsula', and this fits in very well with this route.

And now we encounter a genuine old tradition. Without any introduction, we are suddenly told of a dialogue between Hobab the Midianite and Moses:

And Moses said unto Hobab, the son of Reuel the Midianite, Moses' father-in-law, We are journeying unto the place of which Yahweh said, I will give it you: come thou with us, and we will do thee good: for Yahweh hath spoken good concerning Israel. And he said unto him, I will not go; but I will depart to mine own land, and to my kindred. And he said, Leave us not, I pray thee; forasmuch as thou knowest how we are to camp in the wilderness, and thou mayest be to us instead of eyes. And it shall be, if thou go with us, yea, it shall be, that what goodness Yahweh shall do unto us, the same will we do unto thee [*Numbers 10: 29–32*].

The phrase 'Moses' father-in-law' can be read as applying either to Reuel or to Hobab, which explains why some older commentators have identified Hobab with Jethro and others have claimed that he was Jethro's (otherwise Reuel's) son. There were clearly different traditions about the name and the precise relationship to Moses of the Midianite or Kenite who plays such a significant part in Moses' affairs. In Judges 1: 16 we hear of 'the children of the Kenite, Moses' father-in-law', and in Judges 4: 11 we are told that 'Heber the Kenite, which was of the children of Hobab the father-in-law of Moses, had severed himself from the Kenites'. But the main interest of the passage quoted from Numbers 10 is that it is clear evidence of an old tradition concerning help given to Moses and the Israelites by Midianites or Kenites, whose knowledge of that part of the Sinai peninsula made them invaluable as guides. We are not told what reply Hobab made to Moses' request, but the assumption must be that it was positive, for the passage in Judges shows that there was a whole colony of Kenites among the people of Israel after their entry into Palestine and that they were identified as the people to whom 'Hobab the father-in-law of Moses' belonged. The silence on the part of the narrator with reference to Hobab's reply might perhaps be explained by his realizing that his account of Midianites guiding the Israelites through the wilderness because of their local knowledge was not really compatible with the statement that such guidance was given by Yahweh himself. An emphatic statement to this effect follows immediately after the account of Moses' appeal to Hobab:

And they departed from the mount of Yahweh three days' journey: and the ark of the covenant of Yahweh went before them in the three days' journey, to search out a resting place for them. And the cloud of Yahweh was upon them by day, when they went out of the camp. And it came to pass, when the ark set forward, that Moses said, Rise up, Yahweh, and let thine enemies be scattered; and let them that hate thee flee before thee. And when it rested, he said, Return, Yahweh, unto the many thousands of Israel [Numbers 10: 33–6].

Two traditions are here brought together: Yahweh's guidance by means of the cloud, and the significance of the ark's being carried before the people as they marched. The ark was a symbol of God's presence among the people *in battle,* to give them victory, as is made clear from the words put into Moses' mouth when it set forward and when it rested as well as from the story in Chapter 14 of the Israelites' defeat by Amalekites and Canaanites, when they went to battle against Moses' express command and without taking the ark with them. These words of Moses are clearly ancient. They represent (in their appeal to Yahweh to rise up, at the beginning of a battle) the early concept of the ark, which may well be Moses' own, that it was a representation of the throne or footstool on which the invisible Yahweh rested.

The children of Israel are now marching north, towards the Promised Land (Canaan, or Palestine). They are now properly organized and ready to encounter and defeat any forces that contest their passage. It looks as though the story of the exodus and its consequences will soon be at an end: Moses has brought the people to Sinai and Yahweh has there revealed his commands and promised by covenant to protect and assist them. A few days' marching should bring them to the southern border of Canaan. It is at this point that we are told of a series of rebellious acts which eventually result in God's punishing the people by decreeing that they shall wander in the wilderness for such a

The ark of the covenant: a 16th-century engraving after Petrus Aquila.

long period that none of the generation that set out from Egypt at the age of twenty or over (with two exceptions) shall set foot in the Promised Land.

First we have a brief and somewhat cryptic account of an unexplained complaint by the people and its consequences:

And when the people complained, it displeased Yahweh: and Yahweh heard it; and his anger was kindled; and the fire of Yahweh burnt among them, and consumed them that were in the uttermost parts of the camp. And the people cried unto Moses; and when Moses prayed unto Yahweh, the fire was quenched. And he called the name of the place Taberah: because the fire of Yahweh burnt among them [Numbers 11: 1–4].

What we have here is the tradition of 'murmuring' (the Hebrew word so often translated thus is now thought to have been a technical term used when a vassal breached the terms of a treaty with his superior) linked to an explanation of a place-name by folk etymology. We do not, however, know where

Taberah was, though if it was known to the redactor who was responsible for this passage it must have been in northern Sinai somewhere between Egypt and Palestine and not too far from the border of Palestine. Nor do we know the true etymology of the word: its derivation from the Hebrew *ba'ar*, to burn, is not accepted by modern scholars.

The account of the Taberah incident is immediately followed by an account of complaints about food, part of the same tradition that, as we have noticed, was used in Chapter 16 of Exodus. Here it is stated that the complaint was started by the 'mixed multitude', but it was taken up by all the people. They are now complaining of the monotony of the manna. In a remarkable passage, Moses is represented as reproaching Yahweh for having given him the impossible task of leading these people:

Then Moses heard the people weep throughout their families, every man in the door of his tent: and the anger of Yahweh was kindled greatly; Moses also was displeased. And Moses said unto Yahweh, Wherefore hast thou afflicted thy servant? and wherefore have I not found favour in thy sight, that thou layest the burden of all the people upon me? Have I conceived all this people? have I begotten them, that thou shouldest say unto me, Carry them in thy bosom, as a nursing father [the Hebrew word here is omen, *which means 'nurse' or 'guardian'; though it is masculine in form, and there is a feminine form,* omenet, *it seems to have a maternal rather than a paternal implication here*] *beareth the sucking child, unto the land which thou swarest unto their fathers? Whence should I have flesh to give unto all this people? for they weep unto me, saying, Give us flesh, that we may eat. I am not able to bear all this people alone, because it is too heavy for me. And if thou deal thus with me, kill me, I pray thee, out of hand, if I have found favour in thy sight; and let me not see my wretchedness* [Numbers 11: 10–15].

Three points emerge. Both Yahweh and Moses are angry with the people. Moses blames Yahweh for having laid on him the burden of nursing these refractory children. And he feels unable to carry the burden alone. A fourth point, that if Yahweh cannot do better than this he had better kill him, is a startling rhetorical flourish with which he emphasizes his complaints. This is the only time that we have an image of Moses as a parent or nurse of the children of Israel; the very rarity of the image suggests that it is used in extreme exasperation and it looks therefore as though we have here a genuine tradition of Moses' being driven at one point nearly to despair by the people's lack of discipline and self-control. The complaint about his being unable to bear the burden alone, and God's reply that he should delegate part of his duties to seventy elders, sounds like a version of the story of Moses' need to delegate

The Israelites gathering manna, by Ercole de Roberti.

that we have already seen in the account of the advice given him by Jethro in Chapter 18 of Exodus. But here a new element is added. God tells Moses that he will lay part of the divine spirit, the *ruach*, that is upon Moses when God communes with him, upon the seventy selected elders. Then, after an inserted passage telling how God handled the matter of the people's protests about food, we are told of the spirit descending on the elders so that they 'prophesied' while another two men, who were not among the chosen seventy, also felt the touch of the divine spirit and prophesied. And when Joshua protested to Moses that these two unauthorized men were prophesying, he replied, 'Enviest thou for my sake? would God that all Yahweh's people were prophets, and that Yahweh would put his spirit upon them.'

This seems an odd theme to emerge in relation to the people's complaints about food and Moses' feeling of desperation. Noth, assuming that the reference to the spirit descending and leading the men to prophesy means that they were wrought into a state of ecstasy during which they uttered possibly incomprehensible words, comments that this was a strange way to lighten Moses' burden. He professes to be thoroughly puzzled by the whole episode. It may well be a late insertion whose purpose was to defend the *nebiim*, the prophets, who arose at a later period in Israel's history. Buber sees the descent of the spirit on the elders, connected as it is with the complaints about food, as illuminating 'the antithesis of flesh and spirit'. In his complaint to God Moses had said that he could not carry on alone, and in his reply God showed him that he had not left him unaided for he was present internally as well. Further, Buber argues, the story of Moses' wishing that all the people were prophets is connected with God's earlier command that Israel should be a kingdom of priests, and though the expression of the wish 'is admittedly not Mosaic in the strict sense' it 'may be ascribed to the after-effects of Moses' spirit'.

The Hebrew word for spirit, *ruach*, which is first found in the Bible in the second verse of the first chapter of Genesis, also means 'wind', so when we are told in Numbers 11: 31 'And there went forth a wind from Yahweh and brought quails from the sea' the Hebrew word for 'wind' here is the same as the word translated 'spirit' in the account of the descent of the divine spirit on the elders. There may well be a deliberate juxtaposition of internal and external manifestations of divine activity here, the fact that the same word is used for both being part of the narrator's message, as it were. The quails are brought in not just to meet the people's desire to eat flesh, as happens in the Exodus version of the story, but also as a form of punishment for their disobedience and faithlessness. Yahweh commands Moses to tell the people that since they are crying for flesh Yahweh will indeed give them flesh. 'Ye shall not eat one day, nor two days, nor five days, neither ten days, nor twenty days;

The return of the spies, by A. Strähuber.

but even a whole month, until it comes out at your nostrils, and it be loathsome unto you: because that ye have despised Yahweh which is among you, and have wept before him, saying, Why came we forth out of Egypt?' Later we are told that after the wind blew in the quails so that they fell by the camp in multitudes the people gathered and ate them. 'And while the flesh was yet between their teeth, ere it was chewed, the wrath of Yahweh was kindled against the people, and Yahweh smote the people with a very great plague.' The story may well have a naturalistic explanation. The sudden appearance from the direction of the Mediterranean of a flock of migrating quails, which settled

163

on the ground in large numbers and proved easy to catch, may well have resulted in the people catching and killing many more than they could eat in a short time, so that they kept on eating the birds after they had gone bad.

We next hear of two complaints against Moses which come, surprisingly, from Miriam and Aaron, who are however not here identified as Moses' sister and brother. Moses is reproached for having married a Cushite or Ethiopian woman and then, as though the writer is further exploring the implications of the command that the people should become a nation of priests and Moses' hope that they would all become prophets, they complain about Moses' assumption that he is the sole conveyor of the word of Yahweh: 'And they said, Hath Yahweh indeed spoken only by Moses? hath he not spoken also by us?' The account, in Numbers 12, seems to be a conflation of two separate incidents, Miriam's complaint about Moses' wife and Aaron's jealousy of Moses' unique relationship with Yahweh. We have discussed earlier the significance of the traditions that Moses married a foreign wife. Here there are no details of any kind given, and we are not told whether the objection to the Cushite wife was her colour. But it is perhaps significant that Yahweh punished Miriam for this attack on Moses by turning her 'leprous, white as snow' and her leprosy was only cured on Aaron's intervention (suggesting that Aaron was not himself involved in this attack). Was this an example of Yahwistic irony? Perhaps the implication is: 'She's too dark for you, is she? If you prefer whiteness, I'll make you whiter than ever.' We hear no more of Aaron's complaint, or of any punishment. The only comment made by the narrator on the complaint about Moses' claiming a unique relationship with Yahweh is: 'Now the man Moses was very meek, above all the men which were upon the face of the earth.' The implication seems to be either that the charge was wholly without foundation, since Moses was too meek ever to claim any superiority for himself, or that, since he behaved so meekly, people could be deluded into thinking that they could depose him from his unique position.

The most dramatic of the series of rebellious acts on the part of the children of Israel comes after Moses has sent twelve spies, one from each tribe, to spy out the land of Canaan and report back. Though the report in Numbers 13 seems to be a mixture of two different accounts and contains a number of repetitions and inconsistencies, the outline is clear. They are sent to 'see the land, what it is; and the people that dwelleth therein, whether they be strong or weak, few or many; and what the land is that they dwell in, whether it be good or bad; and what cities they be that they dwell in, whether in tents, or in strongholds; and what the land is, whether it be fat or lean, and whether there be wood therein or not.' The older stratum in the account, attributed to J, sends them through the Negeb to Hebron, where they explored the rich vine-growing district. The later P stratum states that they explored the whole country from north to south. According to J, the spies started out from Kadesh-barnea, where the people were now encamped. Their interest was in only the southern hill country of what was later to be the kingdom of Judah and, arriving at the time of grape-gathering, they brought back a massive cluster of grapes, together with pomegranates and figs, as proof of the land's richness. J includes one of those interesting historical asides that are interspersed throughout the biblical story: 'Now Hebron was built seven years before Zoan in Egypt.' (Zoan, which the Greeks called Tanis, was built on the site of the ancient Hyksos capital Avaris and was the same city as Raamses. The

Corn in the Promised Land.

Fruit from the Promised Land: pomegranates (ABOVE); date palms (BELOW).

point being made is that Hebron was a very ancient town.) The grapes they brought back were gathered from a vineyard in the valley of Eshcol. *Eshkol* is the Hebrew word for 'cluster of grapes', and this 'Grape Valley' must have been in southern Palestine. The cluster they brought back, symbol of the land's fertility, was so big that 'they bare it between two poles upon a staff', a realistic touch that sounds authentic. (The association of Caleb, of the tribe of Judah, in J's narrative with the important city of Hebron at the centre of the wine-producing region of the Judaean mountains shows a genuine old tradition of the taking of Hebron by Calebites at an early stage of the Israelite conquest. The tradition was incorporated into the story by a later redactor looking back from a period in Israelite history when Hebron was in the possession of the Calebites and offering an explanation of this fact.)

The spies, having been away a symbolic forty days, return to report that the land is indeed rich, but it is impregnable.

And they told him, and said, We came unto the land whither thou sentest us, and surely it floweth with milk and honey; and this is the fruit of it. Nevertheless the people be strong that dwell in the land, and the cities are walled, and very great: and moreover we saw the children of Anak there. The Amalekites dwell in the land of the south: and the Hittites, and the Jebusites, and the Amorites, dwell in the mountains: and the Canaanites dwell by the sea, and by the coast of Jordan. And Caleb stilled the people before Moses, and said, Let us go up at once, and possess it; for we are well able to overcome it. But the men that went up with him said, We be not able to go up against the people; for they are stronger than we [Numbers 13: 27–31].

'The children of Anak' (actually, the Hebrew has the definite article before Anak, reading 'the children of the Anak'), who are also referred to in a later verse of the same chapter as *nephilim*, 'giants', described in Genesis 6: 4 as 'mighty men of old . . . men of renown', seems here to mean simply people of unusual size and strength. The Hebrew word *anak* means a necklace and is used in Judges 8: 26 to refer to chains around camels' necks, so the phrase 'the children of the Anak' may mean 'descendants of the necklace people', though what the significance of that is we cannot say. The reference to Hittites is puzzling, because the Hittite empire, which collapsed at the end of the thirteenth century BC, never extended as far southward as Palestine: the term 'Hittite' seems to be used here in a very vague sense. The Jebusites, whose origins are obscure, are mentioned in Joshua as the inhabitants of Jerusalem: it was King David's capture of Jerusalem and his transformation of it into his capital that was

OVERLEAF A view over the hills of Judaea.

eventually to put an end to the Jebusite kingdom. (The account is in Chapter 5 of II Samuel.) The Amorites, a Semitic people or group of peoples who had for centuries inhabited north-western Mesopotamia and northern Syria (they appear as Amurru, 'westerners', in cuneiform texts), seem to have come south from Syria and established a kingdom east of the Jordan, perhaps ruling over Hebrew shepherds and farmers who had not been in Egypt but had migrated from western Palestine. Canaanite city states, each ruled by a 'king', existed throughout Palestine, especially on the coast; they were under nominal Egyptian suzerainty. P's account states in more general terms what we have already read in J's account:

And they brought up an evil report of the land which they had searched unto the children of Israel, saying, The land, through which we have gone to search it, is a land that eateth up the inhabitants thereof; and all the men that we saw in it are men of a great stature. And there we saw the giants, the sons of Anak which come of the giants: and we were in our own sight as grasshoppers, and so we were in their sight [Numbers 13: 32–4].

The result is a massive rebellion on the part of the people. They unanimously declare that it would be better for them to have died in Egypt or in the wilderness rather than that they and their wives and children should fall by the sword, they reproach Yahweh for having brought them to this fate, and they conclude by deciding to appoint a new leader to take them back to Egypt. This time Joshua, as well as Caleb (the latter alone in J's original version had been in favour of undertaking the conquest of the Promised Land) reasserts the goodness of the land and assures the people that Yahweh will be with them and bring them safely into it. But the people will not listen. 'All the congregation bade stone them with stones.'

This must be an echo of a real historical situation. The people are encamped at Kadesh-barnea on the southern approaches to Palestine. This was a great oasis about forty-six miles south-south-west of Beersheba. They spent a long time here – the biblical account says thirty-eight years, having spent two years in wandering before they reached it – and clearly it afforded the people and their animals abundant water and pasture. It may have been during their stay here that they first developed the habits of an agricultural people tilling arable land, and it may have been here too, as Buber suggests, that Moses began to realize fully the social and legal transformations that were necessary if the people were to settle in the Promised Land as arable farmers rather than stock breeders. And it must have been from here that they made the first attempts

Modern Bedouins at the market at Beersheba.

to penetrate Palestine. The lack of success of these attempts, and the realization that they would involve loss in battle in a long and wearisome campaign, must have led to popular disillusionment. To this extent the tradition recorded in Numbers 13–14 is entirely credible. And the story, which follows immediately, of Moses' interceding for the people to avert Yahweh's wrath against them, is yet one more strand in the well attested tradition of Moses' difficulties and eventual success as a leader of a sometimes bewildered people.

After the people threaten to stone Caleb and Joshua, the glory of Yahweh appears in the tabernacle, and Yahweh speaks:

And Yahweh said unto Moses, How long will this people provoke me? and how long will it be ere they believe me, for all the signs which I have showed among them? I will smite them with pestilence, and disinherit them, and will make of thee a greater nation and a mightier than they.

And Moses said unto Yahweh, Then the Egyptians shall hear it, (for thou broughtest up this people in thy might from among them;) And they will tell it to the inhabitants of this land: for they have heard that thou Yahweh art among this people, that thou Yahweh art seen face to face, and that thy cloud standeth over them, and that thou goest before them, by daytime in a pillar of cloud, and in a pillar of fire by night. . . . Pardon, I beseech thee, the iniquity of this people according unto the greatness of thy mercy, and as thou hast forgiven this people, from Egypt even until now. And Yahweh said, I have pardoned according to thy word [Numbers 13: 11–14: 20].

But though they are forgiven, they will still be punished. 'Surely they shall not see the land which I sware unto their fathers, neither shall any of them that provoked me see it.' Only Caleb (and, in P's version, also Joshua) will live to enter the land. As for the others, 'your carcasses shall fall in this wilderness, and all that were numbered of you, according to your whole number, from twenty years old and upward, which have murmured against me.'

The people whom Moses led out of Egypt as a band of fugitive slaves to mould into a nation and prepare for an agricultural life in a new land did not, and could not, storm directly out of Egypt into Palestine. They had to go a long way round, not only to avoid border fortresses but also because they needed time to acquire cohesion and principles. The sense of popular resentment at the discovery that the way from Egypt to a new fertile land was not quick or easy runs through much of the biblical narrative. Why did it have to take so long? The answer developed by the people's own tradition that it was their own fault: they were being punished for their ingratitude and rebelliousness. This tendency to blame all their misfortunes on the people's own sins is one of the most striking characteristics of the Israelite tradition. In later

generations their prophets were to thunder threats against them for disobeying Yahweh's commands, and when eventually they lost their Promised
Land to go into exile the whole people were brought to accept this as just
punishment for their sins. To this day orthodox Jews attribute their two-
thousand-year exile from their ancient homeland as God's punishment for
the sins of their ancestors, but always with the promise of forgiveness and
restoration in the end. Does this attitude go back to the punishment of forty
years' wandering in the wilderness combined with the promise of eventual
entry (for their children) into the Promised Land? If so, is it in origin a Mosaic
concept? We have already noted that the commands promulgated by Moses
in the name of Yahweh had for their objective the secure and prosperous
development of the community: the blessings for obedience are material
blessings and the curses for disobedience are material curses. Was Moses'
response to the discomforts and complaints of his wandering people to
blame themselves for misfortune and at the same time to encourage them to
believe that reformed behaviour on their part would eventually produce
tangible evidence of God's favour? We meet at so many stages in Israel's
history the belief that if the people suffered a national misfortune *it must have
been their own fault* that it is tempting to trace the idea right back to Moses. It
was a way of reconciling the idea of a just and benevolent God with human
suffering. Suffering, especially if undergone on a national scale by the people
whom God had selected to bear the special responsibility of a covenant relationship with him, had to be seen as punishment for disobeying God's will:
only then could it be accepted. The notion that disobedience of God's commands produces suffering easily leads to the notion that suffering is the sign of
the sufferer's guilt. Moses himself never made this inference, or at least there
is no suggestion in the Mosaic books that he did, but it could easily be inferred
from the Mosaic law. It was the author of Job (who lived probably in the fifth
or sixth century BC) who pointed out the dangers of this view: guilt may
eventually produce suffering but a wholly virtuous man may also suffer, for
the universe is constructed in mysterious ways and we cannot fathom the
mysteries of God's intentions. The author of Job is concerned with the problem of individual suffering. Moses was concerned with legislating for a people,
and the reward of obedience to Yahweh promised in the Mosaic books is
national prosperity just as the punishment for disobedience is national disaster.
Yet Moses, as the biblical account repeatedly emphasizes, was a man who
found his deepest insights in solitude. Here then is another paradox about him:
he was essentially a community legislator and as such left an indelible mark on
the character and thought of his people, but the nature of the legislation he
promulgated for the community was revealed to him in mystical isolation.

Immediately after the account of the depressing report of the returned spies and its consequences we get an account of an actual military attempt to conquer territory in southern Palestine which, because of the specificity of its geographical detail, must derive from a genuine penetration of the Israelites into the Negeb. This action is represented as the response of the people to Yahweh's reproaches. They are now eager to push northward into the Promised Land.

And they rose up early in the morning, and gat them up into the top of the mountain, saying, Lo, we be here, and will go up unto the place which Yahweh hath promised: for we have sinned. And Moses said, Where now do ye transgress the commandment of Yahweh? but it shall not prosper. Go not up, for Yahweh is not among you; that ye be not smitten before your enemies. For the Amalekites and the Canaanites are there before you, and ye shall fall by the sword: because ye are turned away from Yahweh, therefore Yahweh will not be with you. But they presumed to go up unto the hilltop: nevertheless the ark of the covenant of Yahweh, and Moses, departed not out of the camp. Then the Amalekites came down, and the Canaanites which dwelt in that hill, and smote them, and discomfited them, even unto Hormah [Numbers 14: 40–5].

This is the report of an unauthorized raid, which was (for that reason) unsuccessful. But in Numbers 21: 1–3 we are told of a great Israelite victory at the same place, Hormah. 'And Yahweh hearkened to the voice of Israel, and delivered up the Canaanites; and they utterly destroyed them and their cities: and he called the place Hormah.' Later still, in Judges 1: 16–17, we find the region inhabited by Kenites and Canaanites, the latter being defeated by the tribe of Judah. What we seem to have here are traditions representing the entrance of a number of different groups from the area around Kadesh. The area is clearly enough defined. Hormah was a few miles south-east of Beersheba, in the hilly country between the arable land and the desert, and here nomadic Amalekites and settled Canaanites united to repel a band of invading Israelites, though a later Israelite invasion was successful. John Bright has warned against over-simplifying the complex problem of Israel's entry into the Promised Land. 'Israel came into being by a process exceedingly complex. Her clan structure was filled out with strains of diverse origin and, we may not doubt, found its normative form only after the settlement in Palestine.' Recent archaeological excavations, while throwing a great deal of light on the history of sites in Palestine, emphasize the complexity of the problems connected with the Israelite conquest.

King Solomon's pillars, in the Negeb desert.

8

In Sight of the Promised Land

The reaction of the people of Israel to the report of the spies is intended to be seen as the climax of their 'murmurings' against Moses and their resistance to his plans for them: the fact that it is followed by Yahweh's punishment of not allowing the original generation to enter the Promised Land suggests this clearly enough. Yet in the biblical account it is not the last of the rebellions against Moses. Chapter 16 of Numbers gives an account of the rebellion of 'Korah, the son of Izhar, the son of Kohath, the son of Levi, and Dathan and Abiram, the sons of Eliab and On, the son of Peleth, sons of Reuben'. They are said to have gathered 'two hundred and fifty princes of the assembly, famous in the congregation, men of renown', and protested that Moses and Aaron were arrogating too much to themselves, 'seeing all the congregation are holy, every one of them, and Yahweh is among them'. Moses reproaches them as 'sons of Levi', pointing out that they have the privilege of doing the service of Yahweh's tabernacle and standing before the congregation to minister to them: do they want the priesthood also? he asks. At this point it is said that it is Aaron (not Moses and Aaron) that they are murmuring against. Moses then summons Dathan and Abiram, but they refuse to come, and accuse Moses of incompetence and overweening ambition. Moses then summons Korah and his group to assemble with their censers full of fire and incense before the door of the tabernacle (a priestly prerogative) and announces that

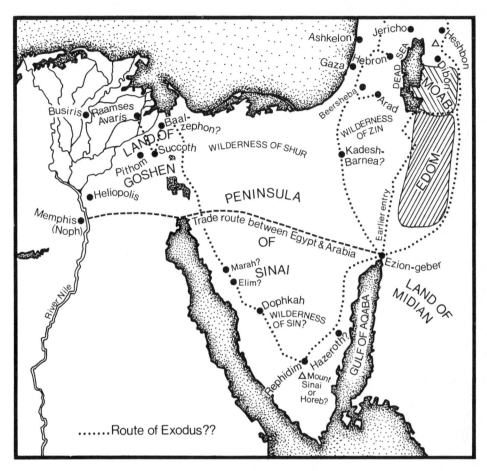

Yahweh will vindicate him. Instead of being allowed to minister with their censers Korah and his men are swallowed up alive into the earth, while 'the two hundred and fifty men that offered incense' (we are not told how they are distinguished from Korah's men who were swallowed up with him) are consumed in a fire sent by Yahweh. The moral, we are told, is 'that no stranger, which is not of the seed of Aaron, come near to offer incense before Yahweh; that he be not as Korah, and as his company'. A plague descends on the people, but Aaron's priestly officiating with a censer brings it to a stop, although not before it had destroyed many people. As for Dathan and Abiram, they too, who had assembled outside their tents with their families to defy Moses, were engulfed in the same convulsion that swallowed up Korah.

OVERLEAF The punishment of Korah, Dathan and Abiram, by Botticelli, from his fresco in the Sistine Chapel.

There is clearly a confusion here of at least two different traditions. The story of Korah, who is presented in Numbers 16: 2 as a leader of two hundred and fifty important men and in verses 8 to 11 as a spokesman for a group of rebellious Levites, must originally have been quite separate from the story of Dathan and Abiram, and is itself probably composed of different strands. Its main strand would seem to reflect a conflict between the Aaronite priesthood and the Levitical family of Korah during the early period of the monarchy, which was read back into the accounts of 'murmurings' against Moses in order to give Mosaic authority to the Aaronite claims and at the same time to make certain points about the true meaning of Moses' claim that Israel was to become a kingdom of priests and his wish that all the people were prophets. The complaints of Dathan and Abiram, of the tribe of Reuben, are much more likely to stem from an older tradition of straightforward rebellion against Moses' leadership.

The Korahites were active during the monarchy as choristers in the Temple: Psalms 42 to 49 are said to be 'for the sons of Korah'. There is other biblical evidence of their importance in public worship during the monarchy (e.g., II Chronicles 20: 19: 'And the Levites, of the children of the Kohathites, and of the children of the Korahites, stood up to praise Yahweh God of Israel with a loud voice on high'). It seems likely that we have in Chapter 16 of Numbers an echo of a later quarrel between the Korahites, dissatisfied with their limited Levitical function, and the Aaronite priests, who considered themselves and their functions to be superior. But the association of the story of Korah with that of Dathan and Abiram and its setting in the wilderness in the context of 'murmurings' against Moses are significant. For what emerges is a probing of the meaning of leadership in the kind of community which Moses welded together and for which he provided divinely authorized legislation. The events as narrated are a crude enough story of rebellion followed by savage punishment, but the implications go much further and may well stem from genuinely Mosaic traditions about the true meaning of Yahweh's choice of Israel for his people. If the divine election meant that Israel was henceforth automatically a holy people, then there was no need of Moses' leadership or his mediating of God's word, and Israel achieved its destiny simply by existing. Or again, since the divine commandments had been promulgated so that everybody now knew them, what need was there for any further mediation? There is a contradiction involved in Moses' meekness, in his proclamation of Yahweh as the one source of moral and cultic imperatives on the one hand, and his role of leader on the other. There is more than one suggestion in the

The death of Korah, Dathan and Abiram, by Doré.

biblical narratives that it was Moses' meekness that provoked rebellion, just as there are suggestions that Yahweh's apparent failure to deliver ease and success at a stroke provoked scepticism about the people's covenant with him. There is a further point. Moses was a political as well as a moral and religious leader, and what might be called his theocratic politics raised questions about the relationship between *Realpolitik* and divine law. Does Chapter 16 of Numbers contain echoes of doubts and confusions on these matters that arose in connection with Moses' own life and work? Buber has argued eloquently that the story of Korah illustrates paradoxes and contradictions that go back to the Mosaic situation itself and reflects problems concerning, for example, the relation between law and freedom that are encountered even by primitive peoples and which have a special dimension in the context of the achievement of Moses. He also points out that Moses and Korah shared a common goal, that Israel should be Yahweh's people, the holy people. 'But for Moses this was the goal. In order to reach it, generation after generation had to choose again and again between the roads, between the way of God and the wrong paths of their own hearts.' He sees Moses as being 'zealous against the great and popular mystical Baal which, instead of demanding that the people should hallow themselves in order to be holy, treats them as already holy' and he sees Korah's crime as wrongly identifying that Baal with Yahweh. This is the tone of the modern preacher developing the implications of a text rather than of the scholar probing for historical reality underlying transmitted traditions, but it may well be that the Korah story, originating as it did in a later quarrel between Levitical and Aaronite elements in the Temple, was set back into a Mosaic context by a redactor who realized that it illuminated some of the problems and conflicts that Moses himself was made aware of in the course of his career as leader and lawgiver.

Numbers follows the account of the rebellion of Korah and of Dathan and Abiram with a chapter of regulations concerning the relation of priests and Levites to the rest of Israel and a chapter on rituals of purification, but as the material here is almost certainly post-Mosaic it need not detain us. The next chapter (20) opens with the death of Miriam and ends with the death of Aaron. Miriam, we are told, died 'when the people abode in Kadesh', and was buried there. This probably embodies a genuine tradition that there was a grave in Kadesh-barnea associated with Miriam and it is the last of the few and unrelated references to Miriam (as Moses' sister, as a prophetess who leads singing women after the victory at the Reed Sea, and as a complainant against Moses for having married a Cushite) scattered throughout Exodus and Numbers. Its insertion at this point, in a section which goes on to explain why Moses too had to die before reaching the Promised Land and ends with the death of Aaron,

The rebellion of Korah: from a 13th-century English psalter.

suggests that the redactor was aware of moving towards the end of the story of the exodus and the wanderings and the deaths of the principal characters in it.

We now get another account of the people's 'murmuring' against Moses for the lack of fruit and of water which echoes almost precisely the account given in Chapter 17 of Exodus and is not appropriate to Kadesh-barnea, which was a great oasis. The only difference between the two accounts is that in this Yahweh tells Moses to take his rod and speak to the rock, and it will give forth water, whereas in the Exodus version he was told to strike it. But instead of speaking to it he strikes it. Water indeed came forth abundantly 'and the congregation drank and their beasts also', but Yahweh was angry with Moses for not having obeyed his instructions to the letter. 'And Yahweh spake unto Moses and Aaron [there is no reason given why Aaron should be involved here], Because ye believed me not, to sanctify me in the eyes of the children of Israel, therefore ye shall not bring this congregation into the land which I have

Moses striking water from the rock, by Jacobo Robusti.

given them.' We are then told that 'this is the water of Meribah; because the children of Israel strove with Yahweh, and he was sanctified in them.' This makes it quite clear that the story here is a 'doublet' of the Exodus story (also located at Meribah), inserted here by P in order to provide a reason why neither Moses nor Aaron reached the Promised Land and also (in the curious remark that Yahweh 'was sanctified in them') to provide an etymology for the name Kadesh (Hebrew *kadash*, 'to be holy').

The implication of God's somewhat cryptic announcement of the punishment in store for Moses (and Aaron) for displaying a lack of faith is that Moses, having on previous occasions used his staff with supernatural effect, felt that he had to use it on this occasion too to achieve the flow of water, even though God specifically told him to speak to the rock and do nothing more. But Chapter 20 of Numbers turns immediately from this to an incident which brings us to the theme of Israel's conquest of the Promised Land:

And Moses sent messengers from Kadesh into the king of Edom. Thus saith thy brother Israel, Thou knowest all the travail that hath befallen us: How our fathers went down into Egypt, as we have dwelt in Egypt a long time; and the Egyptians vexed us, and our fathers: And when we cried unto Yahweh he heard our voice, and sent an angel, and hath brought us forth out of Egypt: and, behold, we are in Kadesh, a city in the uttermost of thy border. Let us pass, I pray thee, through thy country: we will not pass through the fields, or through the vineyards, neither will we drink of the water of the wells: we will go by the king's high way, we will not turn to the right hand nor to the left, until we have passed thy borders. And Edom said unto him, Thou shalt not pass by me, lest I come out against thee with the sword. And the children of Israel said unto him, We will go by the high way; and if I and my cattle drink of thy water, then I will pay for it: I will only, without doing anything else, go through on my feet. And he said, Thou shalt not go through. And Edom came out against him with much people, and with a strong hand. Thus Edom refused to give Israel passage through his border: wherefore Israel turned away from him [Numbers 20: 14–21].

Edomites and Moabites, who were to remain Israel's neighbours throughout her history, had only recently established themselves east of the Jordan, the former in the high country east of the Arabah between the southern end of the Dead Sea and the head of the Gulf of Aqaba and the latter to their immediate north, east of the Dead Sea. They were ruled by kings (the kings who 'reigned in the land of Edom, before there reigned any king over the children of Israel' are listed in Genesis 36: 31–9), but their origins remain obscure. What we have in the passage just quoted from Numbers is the record of a tradition that the Israelites tried to penetrate Palestine from Kadesh-barnea through Edom, and when they found themselves unable to do so were forced to march round Edom and Moab ('to compass the land of Edom' [Numbers 21: 4]; 'compassed the land of Edom and the land of Moab, and came by the east side of the land of Moab' [Judges 11: 18]) and enter the country from the east. As Bright has commented,

their inability to penetrate the land from the south, and their long detour around Edomite and Moabite territory, reflect accurately the difficulty such a group would have had in breaking through at a time when the fringes of arable land had been largely taken up, in the south by Amalekites and others [we have already seen them being repulsed by the Amalekites and Canaanites], in the east by Edom and Moab. The eastern detour accords well . . . with conditions in the thirteenth century [BC], when the frontiers of Edom and Moab had been secured by a line of fortresses.

But there was also another tradition about the Israelites' route from Kadesh-barnea to the Plains of Moab, according to which they marched from Kadesh-barnea to Punon in Edom (Numbers 33: 42), then turned north to 'Ijeabarim, on the border of Moab' (Numbers 33: 44), thence proceeded by Dibon and Nebo on the Moabite plateau and then 'departed from the mountain of Abarim, and pitched in the plains of Moab by Jordan near Jericho' (Numbers 33: 48). This tradition may refer to a different journey undertaken by a different group. Some scholars believe that the journey whose camping sites are given in Numbers 33 was made at an earlier period than the exodus from Egypt led by Moses, before the Edomites and Moabites had established their kingdoms; Noth goes so far as to argue that the itinerary given in this chapter suggests that Mount Sinai lay in north-western Arabia and what we have here is the itinerary of a pilgrim route to and from Sinai, but this view is not generally accepted.

However we interpret the differences between accounts of the route given in Numbers 20 and in Numbers 33, it is clear that the former preserves a genuine tradition about the Israelites' necessity to avoid going through the territory of the kingdoms of Edom and Moab on their way into the Promised Land. The passage contains some contradictions: in verse 17 they say that they will not drink water from a well and in verse 19 they say that if they drink water (which would have to be from a well) they would pay for it. There seems to be here a conflation of the two sources known as J and E. (E is indicated by the remark that they were led out of Egypt by an angel, an unusual reference, paralleled however by the reference to the Angel of God going before the camp in Exodus 14: 19, which is also attributed to E.) The actual request is unambiguous, and sounds historical: they want permission to use the 'king's highway', a level road running north through Edom from Ezion-geber, at the head of the Gulf of Aqaba. This would seem inconsistent with the statement in Numbers 20: 16, 'and, behold, we are in Kadesh, a city in the uttermost of thy border', which suggests both that Kadesh was a city on the western frontier of Edom, whereas it was not a city but a group of wells and was far west of the Edomite border, and that they could move north along the king's highway from Kadesh-barnea, which was geographically impossible. There is a gap in the narrative somewhere. What seems to have happened is that they were forced to move south from Kadesh-barnea to Ezion-geber and then proceed northward along the eastern border of Edom and Moab until they came to the region north of the River Arnon and east of the Jordan. It was from here that they entered the Promised Land.

'And the children of Israel . . . journeyed from Kadesh, and came unto mount Hor' (Numbers 20: 22). It is on Mount Hor, we are then told, that Aaron dies, because he is charged with Moses with having 'rebelled against [Yahweh's] word at the water of Meribah', and like Moses is condemned not to enter the Promised Land. The identity of Mount Hor has been much debated by scholars, and its location on the road between Kadesh and the Arabah is only one of many sites put forward. The whole story may well be an echo of the tradition about the death of Moses preserved at the end of Deuteronomy: Moses too died on a mountain and the children of Israel mourned for him thirty days, as they are said in Numbers 20: 29 to have mourned for Aaron. It is interesting that there is no mention in this account of Aaron's being buried, which suggests that the account is not linked to any local tradition about his burial place of the kind that seems to have arisen with respect to Moses. A quite different tradition about Aaron's death is preserved in Deuteronomy 10: 6, in one of two verses which do not seem to belong to their context at all and which therefore appear to be an interpolated fragment of an otherwise lost account: 'And the children of Israel journeyed from Beeroth of the children of Jaakan to Mosera: there Aaron died and there he was buried.' We do not know where Mosera was.

'And they journeyed from mount Hor by the way of the Reed Sea, to compass the land of Edom: and the soul of the people was much discouraged because of the way' (Numbers 21: 4). The writer of this verse certainly sees Mount Hor as between Kadesh and the head of the Gulf of Aqaba (it is quite clearly the Gulf of Aqaba that is here meant by the term 'Reed Sea') and in fact is spelling out the implications of what we are told in the previous chapter about Edom's refusal to let them use the highway through the country and their consequent necessity of moving south, then east, then north. But just before this, in the first three verses of Chapter 21, we are given a puzzling account of an event presented as Israel's first positive success in their conquest of the Promised Land:

And when the king of Arad, the Canaanite, which dwelt in the south, heard tell that Israel came by the way of the spies; then he fought against Israel, and took some of them prisoners. And Israel vowed a vow unto Yahweh, and said, If thou wilt indeed deliver this people into my hand, then I will utterly destroy their cities. And Yahweh hearkened to the voice of Israel, and delivered up the Canaanites; and they utterly destroyed them and their cities: and he called the name of the place Hormah.

Excavations carried out in the 1960s revealed an early third millennium BC city of Arad in the Negeb east-north-east of Beersheba, but this city was destroyed not later than 2700 BC and the site was not occupied again until the eleventh century BC. In Judges 1 : 16 we are told of a Kenite settlement there, probably in the eleventh century; in the tenth century a strong citadel was built on its site. But this story leaves Arad an unoccupied site precisely at the time when the Israelites were beginning their occupation of Palestine in the middle of the thirteenth century BC. Further, Arad and Hormah (a few miles south-east of Beersheba) are far from the route from Kadesh-barnea to Ezion-geber which the Israelites took after the refusal of the king of Edom to let them go through the king's highway through his country. The passage does not therefore belong in its context, and the name Arad must be a later insertion. If in fact we eliminate the phrase 'the king of Arad' and take 'the Canaanite' to be a collective noun meaning 'the Canaanites' – and 'Canaanites' was often used as a general term to denote the pre-Israelite inhabitants of Palestine – we get an account of a repulse of the Israelites by the Canaanites followed by an Israelite victory over Canaanites at Hormah. The account is offered as an explanation of the name Hormah (or Chormah), which is derived from the Hebrew word *cherem* which means 'curse' or 'doom of extermination'; certain cities conquered by the invading Israelites were put under the ban and condemned to utter extermination together with all their inhabitants and all their contents. We have already been told in Numbers 14: 45 that Hormah was where Amalekites and Canaanites defeated the Israelites after they had made an invasion from Kadesh-barnea unauthorized by Moses and unaccompanied by the ark. The relationship between the two events set at Hormah is not clear, but the three references to Hormah in Numbers and Judges may well, as Bright has suggested, reflect 'the entrance of various groups directly from the wilderness about Kadesh'. The fact that Moses is not mentioned at all in the account of the victory at Hormah, when it is just the sort of thing that we should expect to be attributed to his leadership, suggests that Numbers 21: 1–3 comes from a non-Mosaic or post-Mosaic tradition. The intrusive nature of these three verses becomes obvious when immediately afterwards we turn once again to the familiar story of 'murmurings' against Moses.

The people complain that they have been brought out of Egypt to die in the wilderness, 'for there is no bread, neither is there any water; and our soul loatheth this light bread'. This time their rebelliousness is punished by fiery

Silver figurines representing deities of the Canaanite-Phoenician pantheon, *c.* 18th–17th century BC, found during excavations at Nahariya.

OVERLEAF *The Brazen Serpent*, by Rubens.

serpents sent by Yahweh; they 'bit the people; and much people of Israel died'. The people then repent, and ask Moses to intercede for them so that Yahweh will remove the serpents. 'And Moses prayed for the people. And Yahweh said unto Moses, Make thee a fiery serpent, and set it upon a pole: and it shall come to pass, that every one that is bitten, when he looketh upon it, shall live. And Moses made a serpent of brass, and put it upon a pole; and it came to pass, that if a serpent had bitten any man, when he beheld the serpent of brass, he lived' (Numbers 21: 5–9).

This strange story combines a number of themes. Firstly, there is the association of the wilderness with venomous snakes and similar dangerous creatures: '. . . who led thee through the great and terrible wilderness, wherein were fiery serpents and scorpions, and drought, where there was no water . . .' (Deuteronomy 8: 15). We think too of Isaiah's references to such creatures: 'for out of the serpent's root shall come forth a cockatrice, and his fruit shall be a fiery flying serpent' (14: 29); 'into the land of trouble and anguish, from whence come the young and old lion, the viper and fiery flying serpent' (30: 6). Secondly, there is the reference in II Kings 18: 4: '[King Hezekiah] removed the high places, and brake the images, and cut down the groves, and brake in pieces the brazen serpent that Moses had made: for unto those days the children of Israel did burn incense to it: and he called it Nehushtan.' Thirdly, there is the widespread ancient association of the serpent with healing and life-giving forces and its use in primitive religions as symbol of sex and death or of death and rebirth, and similar conjunctions of opposites. (This is the concept taken over by the Greeks in the caduceus, the staff with entwined snakes, and in the association of the snake with Asclepius, the god of healing.) What we have in this story would seem to be a combination of a tradition of hardships encountered in the wilderness, including venomous snakes and other deadly creatures, the recurring theme of complaints by the people against Moses, the veneration in the post-Mosaic period of a bronze (a more accurate rendering than 'brass') serpent attributed to or somehow associated with Moses, and the concept of the snake as a symbol of healing. There is also an element of verbal association bound up in the story: *nachash* is Hebrew for 'snake'; *n'choshet* is Hebrew for 'copper' or 'bronze'; and the word *n'chustan* ('Nehushtan') seems to be made up of the Hebrew words for 'snake' and for 'bronze'. Although a later age appears to have worshipped the bronze serpent, which was why Hezekiah destroyed it, there is no suggestion in the Numbers account of image worship. There it is Yahweh who decides that he will heal the people in this way, and the people who looked on the serpent and were healed by it were showing their obedience to Yahweh. Nevertheless the tradition of the serpent as symbol of life and healing must lie behind this story at some level. It is impossible to tell how it came to take its present form and what if any historical association the story has with Moses.

We emerge into something closer to history in Numbers 21 : 21–5:

And Israel sent messengers unto Sihon king of the Amorites, saying, Let me pass through thy land: we will not turn into the fields, or into the vineyards; we will not drink of the waters of the well: but we will go along by the king's high way, until we be past thy borders. And Sihon would not suffer Israel to pass through his border: but gathered all his people together, and went out against Israel into the wilderness; and he came to Jahaz, and fought against Israel. And Israel smote him with the edge of the sword, and possessed his land from Arnon unto Jabbok, even unto the children of Ammon: for the border of the children of Ammon was strong. And Israel took all these cities: and Israel dwelt in all the cities of the Amorites, in Heshbon, and in all the villages thereof.

The same message is sent to Sihon as was sent to the king of Edom, though this time it is Israel rather than Moses who is said to have sent the message. (What the significance, if any, of this difference may be is difficult to say.) Sihon appears to have ruled the territory between the Arnon (which flows

Moses and the brazen serpent: a relief by Vincenzio Daddi.

into the Dead Sea) and the Jabbok (a tributary of the Jordan), and the Israelite victory gave them possession of this. The Ammonites ('even unto the children of Ammon') lived north of the Jabbok. The conquered territory included the important city of Heshbon, which lies north-west of the Dead Sea about fifty miles east of Jerusalem.

The attack on Sihon was apparently made by the Israelites who had moved north from Ezion-geber along the eastern boundaries of Edom and Moab. We have already noted Bright's view that Sihon's Amorite kingdom, which had been established a generation or so previously by Amorites from Syria, included Hebrew farmers and shepherds who had migrated from western Palestine. 'It is possible', Bright argues, 'that when the Israelites appeared in their neighbourhood, these Hebrews, galvanized by the new faith, of which they had surely heard, welcomed the newcomers as potential liberators and deserted Sihon in such numbers that he was left with only his few professional troops to support him; these having been dealt with, they opened the land to Israel – indeed, became themselves Israelites.' This is of course no more than speculation, but it may explain why some towns in central Palestine are later included among those occupied by Israel without any account of military action necessary for the occupation. Though the kingdom of Sihon (which included territory conquered by Sihon from Moab) was assigned to the tribe of Reuben and remained Israelite until it was reconquered by Mesha, king of Moab, in the ninth century BC, it cannot have been regarded by the biblical writers as strictly a part of the Promised Land, since Moses, who had been told he would not enter the Promised Land, died there, and the Deuteronomist who records his death calls the territory the land of Moab. This need not mean that the conquest of Sihon's territory was achieved after the death of Moses, for if the Israelites had not conquered the Amorite territory in the midst of which Moses died, how could they have been in it?

The account of the capture of Heshbon, the capital of Sihon's kingdom, is followed by the introduction of an ancient song, which was known to the writer of this narrative and is inserted here as an appropriate illustration of the events he has been describing. But the song describes a successful attack not on Sihon's Amorite kingdom but on Moab. This is explained by the writer in a preliminary sentence: 'For Heshbon was the city of Sihon the king of the Amorites, who had fought against the former king of Moab, and taken all his land out of his hand, even unto the Arnon. Wherefore they that speak in proverbs say . . .' and here follows the song. He is trying to explain why a song of victory over Moab should be presented as a song of victory over Sihon. But though the 'we' of the third stanza of the song must refer to the Israelites, it is still puzzling why a song of Amorite triumph over Moabites should have been absorbed into Israelite tradition. The explanation put forward by G.E.Mendenhall and accepted by Bright is that Hebrew troops took part in this invasion of northern Moab before the arrival of the Israelites led by Moses, and the amalgamation of the traditions of those Hebrews who had come from Egypt and those who had remained in Palestine gave the Israelite tradition embodied in this song. This is further evidence in support of Bright's view that the conquest of Palestinian cities by the incoming Israelites was aided by Hebrews who had not gone to Egypt but remained in Palestine while recognizing kinship with those who had participated in the exodus.

Here is the song:

> Come into Heshbon,
> Let the city of Sihon be rebuilt and prepared.
> For a fire went out from Heshbon,
> A flame from the city of Sihon:
> It consumed Ar of Moab,
> And the lords of the high places of Arnon.

> Woe to thee, Moab!
> Thou art ruined, O people of Chemosh:
> He hath made his sons fugitives
> And his daughter captives [of Sihon, king] of the Amorites.

> We have shot at them, Heshbon is perished even unto Dibon,
> And we have laid waste even unto Nophah
> Which reacheth unto Medeba.

(The words in square brackets in stanza three seem to be a later addition, for they spoil the rhythm and structure of the original Hebrew. Something has happened, too, to the last stanza, which is overloaded, and the translation of its first line is dubious. We have adopted the Authorized Version rendering with a few modifications.)

The account in Numbers 21 of the defeat of Sihon is followed immediately by an account of the defeat of Og, king of Bashan, which is taken from the longer account of the same victory in the third chapter of Deuteronomy. Bashan lay north-east of the Jordan Valley, east of Lake Kinneret (Sea of Galilee), and was known for the fertility of its volcanic soil. This time Moses is credited with the victory, which took place at Edrei. Edrei and Ashtaroth were Og's two main cities and are mentioned among other cities of Bashan in Egyptian documents of the Middle and New Kingdoms. The defeat of Og entered forcefully into Israelite traditions and it is mentioned many times as a conspicuous example of God's favour. He was said to belong to a race of giants and Deuteronomy 3: 11 describes his enormous bedstead. He is mentioned in Joshua 13: 12 as having been defeated by Moses: 'All the kingdom of Og in Bashan, which reigned in Ashtaroth and in Edrei, who remained of the remnant of the giants: for these did Moses smite, and cast them out.' But in spite of these and other references the historical facts underlying the biblical account cannot be precisely determined. The presence of Moses so far north is not reconcilable with the strong tradition of his having died in the land of Moab.

The Israelites were now in the Plains of Moab, that is in that part of Moab which lies north of the River Arnon and which they had taken from Sihon. The Moabites to the south of them were in a state of panic. We can imagine the effect on the settled peoples of Palestine and Transjordan of the irruption of these Israelites from the desert, toughened by many years of spartan living in the wilderness, inspired by their leader with a confidence that their God was with them and had promised them this land, proclaiming a stern moral code vouchsafed to them by divine revelation, a code which viewed the practices of the Canaanites and others – especially those associated with sexual fertility rituals and the worship of images – as abominations to be rooted out. This is not to say that the Israelites burst out of the wilderness in a single overwhelming rush, carrying all before them. As we have seen, the traditions preserved in the biblical account make it clear that they had to make detours, that more than one group was involved, and, possibly, that they were assisted by kindred people in the cities they were attacking. Nevertheless they were possessed of the Mosaic idea: that they had been liberated from Egypt by Yahweh, that they had a special relationship with him, and that he had revealed to them a code of behaviour, both ethical and ritual, that they were bound by covenant to obey. The fact that Moses himself is not shown as having lived to participate in the conquest of the Promised Land proper may well reflect, as well as the historical fact that the leader of the fugitives from Egypt who welded them into a people and gave them divinely sanctioned laws lived and died before the real conquest of Palestine was begun, the belief that the stern and bloody business of conquering a country, even if done in the implementation of a divine promise and in the interests of a divinely ordained way of life, was not the job of the lawgiver himself. Moses could direct the attack on the Amalekites when they fell on the people's straggling rearguard early in their journeyings from Egypt, but the conquest of Canaanite cities and the application to some of them at least of the practice of *cherem*, 'total

OPPOSITE The worship of the golden calf, from the *Haggadah* illustrated by Ben Shahn.

OVERLEAF Detail from Michelangelo's painting of the bronze serpent in the Sistine Chapel.

Et perdes omnes qui tribulant animā
meam quoniam ego seruus tuus sum.
Gloria patri et filio ⁊ spiritui sancto.
Sicut erat in principio et nunc ⁊ semp.
⁊ in secula seculorum amen. antiphona.
Ne reminiscaris domine delicta mea ul'
pencatum meorum. neq̃ uindictam. su
mas de peccatis meis.

Expliciunt septem psalmi penitentiales.

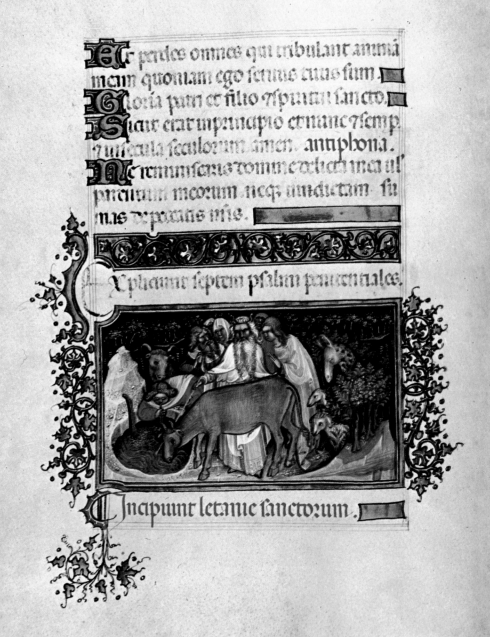

Incipiunt letanie sanctorum.

destruction', was another matter. We are reminded of a tradition concerning a later phase of Israel's history – that King David wanted to build a Temple to the Lord, but the Lord considered that David's career had been too blood-stained (even though his wars were necessary) and would not allow him to do so, leaving it for the peace-loving Solomon to build the Temple.

The panic of the Moabites is clearly expressed in Numbers 22: 1–6:

And the children of Israel set forward, and pitched in the plains of Moab on this side Jordan by Jericho [i.e., they descended to the east bank of the lower Jordan valley, opposite Jericho]. And Balak son of Zippor saw all that Israel had done to the Amorites. And Moab was sore afraid of the people, because they were many: and Moab was distressed because of the children of Israel. And Moab said unto the elders of Midian, Now shall this company lick up all that are round about us, as the ox licketh up the grass of the field. And Balak the son of Zippor was king of the Moabites at that time. He sent messengers therefore unto Balaam the son of Beor to Pethor . . . to call him, saying, Behold, there is a people come out from Egypt: behold, they cover the face of the earth, and they abide over against me. Come now therefore, I pray thee, curse me this people; for they are too mighty for me: peradventure I shall prevail, that we may smite them, and that I may drive them out of this land. . . .

The king of Moab hires a professional soothsayer to pronounce a magical curse on the Israelites. There follows the detailed story of how Balaam is prevented by Yahweh's command from pronouncing the curse. First he re-fuses to go at all; then at Balak's further insistence he goes, and when he arrives at a place from which he can see the Israelite camp spread out before him, he speaks eloquent words of blessing, put into his mouth by Yahweh, instead of the curse he has been hired to pronounce. So Balak was frustrated.

Now clearly there is a great deal of folk material here. Some of the details of the Balaam story, such as the account of his ass stopping because it sees the angel whom Balaam himself cannot see and the dialogue between Balaam and the ass, derive from sources that cannot have anything to do with Moses. And Moses himself is not mentioned in what Buber calls the 'folk-book' of Balaam. We can nevertheless get a glimpse of history behind it. 'After the first great victories over Sihon', Albright has written, 'converts may well have flocked to join the triumphant standards of the new faith. Among them was the Syrian diviner, Balaam, to whose brief conversion we owe the oracles which have been transmitted to us in fragmentary form in Numbers 23–24.' But we can go further than this. Archaeological discoveries have shown that 'Balaam'

Moses strikes water from the rock: from the Codex Landau.

is a well attested North-west Semitic name, paralleled in the name of the Canaanite town of Bileam (1 Chronicles 6: 70) or Ibleam (Joshua 17: 11 and Judges 1: 27), some eight miles south-west of Mount Gilboa. Pethor, where Balaam lived, has been identified as a town in northern Syria. Balaam's role as a professional diviner has been shown (by Samuel Daiches, an uncle of the present writer) to be analogous to that of the Old Babylonian *bārūm*, and a cuneiform seal of a West Semitic *bārūm*, called *Manum*, has been found by archaeologists in a thirteenth-century BC stratum at Beth-Shean. And we know from Mari texts that the *bārūm* was expected to predict the outcome of military operations. The oracles delivered by Balaam – the blessings he uttered instead of the expected curses – are archaic in form and language, and must have been long preserved in oral tradition. So it is reasonable to suppose that we have in the Balaam story, among other elements, a genuine echo of a Syrian diviner converted to the worship of Yahweh and an appreciation of the role of Israel, during the final period of Moses' life when he and his people were in Transjordan poised for entry into the Promised Land proper. 'How godly are thy tents, O Jacob, and thy tabernacles, O Israel,' Balaam exclaimed when he first looked down on the Israelite camp. And later he said: 'He [God] hath not beheld iniquity in Jacob, neither hath he seen perverseness in Israel: Yahweh his God is with him, and the shout of a king is among them.' 'By this,' comments Buber, 'Balaam praises Israel because [Yahweh] their God is with them; and by this the poet once again takes up the old motif of the Annuncia-tion to Moses, the motif of the meaning of God's name.... What he has in mind cannot be anything other than Moses' idea of Israel.' The reference to 'the shout of a king' is to the shout of acclaim for Yahweh the king, the *melech*, of Israel, as set forth in the covenant, mediated by Moses, between Israel and Yahweh. In Chapter 31 of Numbers we are told that Balaam defected to the Midianites, who were now warring against the Israelites; it is as though he had had a glimpse of the Mosaic vision, which he was unable to sustain.

Conversion was not always a one-way affair. Immediately after the story of Balaam we are told that the Israelites, when they 'abode in Shittim' (on the eastern bank of the lower Jordan valley, where they were at the time of the Balaam episode), 'began to commit whoredom with the daughter of Moab'. Their proximity to the Moabites led first to association with Moabite women and then to engaging in Moabite cultic practices. 'And they called the people unto the sacrifice of their gods: and the people did eat, and bowed down to their gods.' Yahweh's anger is kindled, and he summons Moses to punish the offenders by death. A particularly offensive action was the parading by an Israelite called Zimri, of the tribe of Simeon, of his Midianite mistress 'in the sight of Moses, and in the sight of all the congregation of Israel'. Phinehas,

Aaron's grandson, slew them both, thus earning Yahweh's approval and confirmation of 'an everlasting priesthood' for him and his descendants. (This strongly suggests a late tradition, introduced in favour of the Aaronite priesthood and succession.) The terms Moabite and Midianite are used in this section almost interchangeably: Moab is evidently assumed to be under Midianite suzerainty. With no reference to Moses' own relationship by marriage with the Midianites and his friendship with Jethro and others, Yahweh now tells Moses to 'vex the Midianites and smite them', since they are responsible for leading the people astray to worship false gods. Henceforth the Midianites appear in the biblical story as the enemy of Israel, until they are defeated by Gideon at Karkir in the time of the Judges (Judges 8: 10), after which they fade out of Israelite history. This whole section (Number 25) is made up of diverse material some of which goes back to a very early period, but other parts, such as the punishment of Zimri and his mistress by Phinehas and the injunction to war against the Midianites, are of a later date.

There follows yet another census of men of military age, parallel to that in Chapter 1 of Numbers. This leads into the matter of the apportionment of the Promised Land among the tribes, after which we are shown Moses adjudicating on the question of the inheritance of women with no brothers. (Yahweh tells Moses that if a man has no sons his inheritance shall pass to his daughters.) Then, immediately following this decision and with no preparation, we get an intimation of Moses' death:

And Yahweh said unto Moses, Get thee up into this mount Abarim, and see the land which I have given unto the children of Israel. And when thou hast seen it, thou also shalt be gathered to thy people, as Aaron thy brother was gathered. For ye rebelled against my commandment in the desert of Zin, in the strife of the congregation, to sanctify me at the water before their eyes: that is the water of Meribah in Kadesh in the wilderness of Zin [Numbers 27: 12–14].

This appears to be the original version of the narrative, attributed to P, which reappears in Deuteronomy 32: 49–52 with some additions ('. . . unto this mountain Abarim, unto mount Nebo, which is in the land of Moab, that is over against Jericho . . .'). Deuteronomy also emphasizes in the final sentence of its account that Yahweh specifically promises Moses that he shall see, though not enter, the Promised Land: 'Yet thou shalt see the land before thee; but thou shalt not go thither unto the land which I give the children of Israel.' But we shall look later at the significance of the Deuteronomic narrative as a whole.

The account in Numbers then goes on to present Moses asking Yahweh to 'set a man over the congregation, which may go out before them, and which may go in before them, and which may lead them out, and which may bring them in; that the congregation of Yahweh be not as sheep which have no shepherd'. And Yahweh tells Moses to appoint 'Joshua the son of Nun, a man in whom is the spirit'. It is interesting that while the priesthood is set up as hereditary, the leadership of the people is not. It is not one of Moses' sons, but Joshua the son of Nun, who becomes Moses' successor.

The narrative is now interrupted by laws concerning festival offerings and concerning the making and keeping of vows. Then in Numbers 31: 1–2 Yahweh says to Moses: 'Avenge the children of Israel of the Midianites: afterwards shalt thou be gathered unto thy people.' There follows an account of a successful campaign against the Midianites which is very vague and seems to be a late addition. But the following chapter (32), which gives an account of the distribution of land east of the Jordan, is much more likely to embody genuine old traditions. It tells how the tribes of Reuben and Gad, who were predominantly small cattle-breeders, asked Moses' permission to take possession of the good grazing land east of the Jordan. Did this mean, Moses asked in some concern, that they proposed to stay east of the Jordan while their kinsmen went into battle on the other side to gain the Promised Land? No, they replied, they will build sheepfolds for their sheep and walled towns for their dependants, but they themselves will co-operate in the fighting west of the Jordan and only return to their families on the eastern side after the fighting is over. To which Moses replies that if they will really keep this promise 'and will go all of you armed over Jordan before Yahweh, until he hath driven out his enemies from before him and the land be subdued before Yahweh', then indeed they can return without guilt and possess the land east of the Jordan 'before Yahweh'. This has the ring of a genuine historical argument and a genuine compromise.

Chapter 33 of Numbers contains an impressively long list of the various camping places of the Israelites during their journeyings, and the searcher for the underlying history approaches it with excitement, only to discover that many of the names occur nowhere else and are quite unidentifiable. It is a composite list, and, as we have noted earlier, includes what may be information about a route taken by an earlier group than that led by Moses. This chapter concludes with an injunction from Yahweh through Moses to the people that 'ye shall drive out all the inhabitants before you, and destroy all their pictures, and destroy all their molten images, and quite pluck down their high places: And ye shall dispossess the inhabitants of the land, and dwell therein: for I have given you the land to possess it.' How far Moses him-

The Plains of Moab.

Moses viewing the Promised Land, by Sir Frederick Leighton, from Dalziel's *Bible Gallery*, 1880.

self was involved in the practicalities of this policy remains, as we have already suggested, doubtful. The passage just quoted is thought to be late. But there can be no doubt that this was a Holy War of Yahweh and, while the *cherem* was only applied to selected cities that resisted, the conquest – as archaeological evidence confirms – was a violent and bloody business.

There follow more instructions about the division of the land among the tribes (by lot) and the delimitation of its boundaries, again presented as

Yahweh's words to Moses. Chapter 35 deals with the special problem of the Levites, who have no tribal land, and the naming of six of the cities to be given to the Levites as cities of refuge, where an involuntary murderer may find safety until his trial. A careful distinction is drawn, with examples, between involuntary and voluntary killing: only deliberate and premeditated murder is a capital crime, and the man who commits this cannot buy himself off. 'Moreover ye shall take no satisfaction for the life of a murderer, which is guilty of death: but he shall be surely put to death.' Murder pollutes the land, 'and the land cannot be cleansed of the blood that is shed therein, but by the blood of him that shed it.' It would be the grossest injustice, in the Mosaic view of things, for someone other than the murderer to try and expiate the crime by offering his own life. There is no reason for not attributing this view to Moses himself: it is a central part of the Mosaic creed. Nothing could be further from the Mosaic view of divine justice than the words Milton, in Book III of *Paradise Lost*, puts into God's mouth after the fall of Adam:

> He with his whole posterity must die.
> Die he or Justice must; unless for him
> Some other able, and as willing, pay
> The rigid satisfaction, death for death.

The notion that so long as *somebody* suffers, guilty or innocent, justice is done, runs counter to the whole spirit of the Mosaic law. The doctrine of vicarious atonement is equally foreign to it: a symbolic scapegoat might carry the sins of the people away into the wilderness, but no individual could or should cleanse another person of guilt by allowing himself to be punished instead. On this point the Mosaic tradition emphatically differs from the Christian. But it should be remembered that the Mosaic code includes the command to 'love thy neighbour as thyself' and to assist the widow, the fatherless and the stranger. Moses would not have put it this way, but the Mosaic view was that love should co-exist with justice but not corrupt it.

It may not be accidental that this central point about personal responsibility and liability is inserted into Numbers just at the point when Moses is awaiting death and the children of Israel are in Transjordan poised to cross the river and conquer the Promised Land.

9

The Mosaic Tradition

One of the paradoxes faced by anyone who tries to peer through the mists of
the traditions preserved in the Bible to see if he can discover the features of the
historical Moses is that the one biblical book which is attributed to Moses by
a passage of its own text is the one Mosaic book which was almost certainly
produced late in the seventh century BC and is in style and structure quite
unlike the other Mosaic books. It is presented as the testament delivered to the
people by Moses before dying, his farewell speech. Moses is described as
delivering this speech or series of speeches in the land of Moab just before the
Israelite breakthrough into the Promised Land. This is of course clearly a
fiction, as is abundantly proved by internal evidence but, as von Rad has
observed, 'it is surely a very interesting fact that the Israel of the later period of
the monarchy saw itself in the guise, which had become almost canonical, of
the Israel of the Mosaic period.' Von Rad goes on to point out that this is far
removed from a freely chosen literary artifice: 'it is the form in which Israel
presented itself before God, in which it understood itself as the recipient of his
plan of salvation and of his instructions.' That Israel saw in the Mosaic traditions something so fundamental to its national and religious life is a tribute to
the strength of those traditions. But our interest here is not so much in how
strong they were but how reliable. Deuteronomy patently uses a considerable

208

amount of material from the earlier Mosaic books, especially the so-called
Book of the Covenant in Exodus 21–3. There is repetition, modification and
in some cases expansion of selected material from both Exodus and Numbers.
Did the Deuteronomist have access to independent traditions, going back to
the time of Moses, in the light of which some at least of the distinguishing
material in his account can be accepted as genuinely Mosaic? Does, for example, Deuteronomy's emphasis on social legislation from what might be
called a humanistic point of view, his disregard of priestly sources and mini-
mizing of the sacral element to give wherever possible a humanly reasonable
explanation even of a cultic commandment (such as that one should rest on
the sabbath so that one's servants can get a chance to rest, not because God
rested after creating the world in six days) reflect a Mosaic tradition that had
become overlaid by later priestly elements; or does it represent a new development? In some cases the changes must clearly be the result of a changed social
and political situation. The characteristic style of Deuteronomy – lucid, fast-
moving and rhetorical without being ornamental – is certainly late. Nevertheless there is no reason to suppose that everything in Deuteronomy that is
not a mere repetition of what is found in one of the other Mosaic books is
non-Mosaic. The procedure laid down in Chapter 21 in the case of someone
discovered murdered by an unknown assailant bears the marks of the greatest
antiquity. And although there are instructions for electing a king (Chapter
17), there is no mention of a king in any of the Deuteronomic laws relating to
civil institutions and judicial procedure: justice is administered by elders at
the gate. So this sophisticated literary document must have drawn on ancient
material even in some of those sections in which it differs from anything found
in the other Mosaic books. They cannot, of course, always be identified. But
this does not mean that we can eliminate Deuteronomy in any search for traces
of the historical Moses. After all, the other Mosaic books also developed in the
form in which we know them centuries after Moses' time and embodied oral
as well as written traditions descending from earlier periods. Modern scholars
believe that oral traditions continued, though on a diminishing scale, well
into the sixth century BC and the Deuteronomist may well have had access to
some that have not surfaced in the other accounts. It is frustrating to have to be
so tentative on such matters, but tentativeness is inevitable in this kind of
'conjectural history'.

It is now, we are told in Deuteronomy 1:3, 'the fortieth year, in the eleventh
month, on the first day of the month'. The forty years of wandering in the
wilderness are almost over. There is no clear indication anywhere in the Bible

OVERLEAF Raphael's painting of the entry of the Israelites into Canaan.

of exactly how those forty years were spent, though in Deuteronomy 2: 14 we are told that it took thirty-eight years 'from Kadesh-barnea until we were come over the brook Zered' (in Transjordan). The time is specified also in terms of events: it is after the defeat of Sihon, king of the Amorites, and Og, king of Bashan. And so Moses' speech is introduced: 'On this side Jordan, in the land of Moab, began Moses to declare this law . . .'

Moses' speech opens with a fast moving recapitulation, delivered in the first person, of events since the people's departure from Mount Sinai. It differs at some points from what we have been told earlier. Yahweh's refusal to allow Moses to enter the Promised Land is not here connected with the incident of striking the rock for water instead of speaking to it as is recorded in Numbers, but Moses says simply: 'Also Yahweh was angry with me for your sakes, saying, Thou shalt not go in thither.' The Moabites are not represented as refusing passage to the Israelites, but the Israelites avoid going through Moab because Yahweh tells them: 'Distress not the Moabites, neither contend with them in battle: for I will not give thee their land for a possession,' an interesting indication that the passage was written after Moab had regained its independence in the ninth century BC; the writer is acknowledging and explaining this in terms of the old tradition that the Israelites deliberately by-passed Moab in their journeyings. This, and similar passages relating to territories inhabited by other peoples, may represent later additions to the original form of Moses' speech. We get a much fuller account of Og and his kingdom than the perfunctory mention in Numbers (itself probably a late addition), which seems to incorporate a genuine old tradition of a campaign undertaken considerably further north than that against Sihon. (We have already noted, in the previous chapter, the difficulty of assuming that Moses himself was ever in this northern region.) We are given also an expanded version, apparently from an independent source, of Moses' permission to those tribes who had settled in Transjordan (east of the river) to leave their families and cattle there while they co-operated in the conquest west of the river before returning to their homes. We saw it first in Numbers 32: now it is narrated in more general terms:

And I commanded you at that time, saying, Yahweh your God hath given you this land to possess it: ye shall pass over armed before your brethren the children of Israel, all that are meet for the war. But your wives, and your little ones, and your cattle (for I know that ye have much cattle) shall abide in your cities which I have given you; Until Yahweh have given rest unto your brethren, as well as unto you, and until they also possess the land which Yahweh your God hath given them

The Codex Sinaiticus, from the monastery of St Catherine, but now in the British Museum. It is one of the oldest bibles in the world, dating from the first half of the 4th century AD.

beyond Jordan: and then shall ye return every man unto his possession, which I have given you [Deuteronomy 3: 18–20].

Moses goes on to give an account, which occurs nowhere else, of his pleading with God to be allowed to enter the Promised Land, and God's persistence in his refusal. It is of course a literary invention, but one which embodies a strong tradition that the great leader never himself crossed into the country to which he was leading the people. This tradition is confirmed by the traditional location of Moses' grave, 'in a valley in the land of Moab, over against Beth-peor'.

And I besought Yahweh at that time, saying, O my Lord Yahweh, thou hast begun to show thy servant thy greatness, and thy mighty hand: for what God (el) is there in heaven or in earth that can do according to thy works, and according to thy might? I pray thee, let me go over, and see the good land that is beyond Jordan, that goodly mountain, and Lebanon. But Yahweh was wrath with me for your sakes, and would not hear me: and Yahweh said unto me, Let it suffice thee; speak no more unto me of this matter. Get thee up into the top of Pisgah, and lift up thine eyes westward, and northward, and southward, and eastward, and behold it with thine eyes: for thou shalt not go over this Jordan. But charge Joshua, and encourage him, and strengthen him: for he shall go over before this people, and he shall cause them to inherit the land which thou shalt see [Deuteronomy 3: 23–8].

With Chapter 4 of Deuteronomy we come to the recital of the law by the lawgiver himself, preceded by the hortatory sentence, 'Now therefore hearken, O Israel, unto the statutes and unto the judgments, which I teach you, for to do them, that ye may live, and go in and possess the land which Yahweh God of your fathers giveth you'. This suggests a formal opening to a ritual public recital which may have been the way in which the essentials of the Mosaic law were transmitted. But there is something else of interest here too. The second verse continues: 'Ye shall not add unto the word which I command you, neither shall ye diminish aught from it, that ye may keep the commandments of Yahweh your God which I command you.' This is the first suggestion we have in the Bible of a canonical text. Von Rad has pointed out that this 'canonical formula' has a long history, and 'appears as an injunction for scribes as early as in ancient Egypt (Ptah-hotep, *c.* 2450 BC)', so here it may well go back to a Mosaic origin. Moses now goes on to recall the events at Sinai (here called Horeb) and gives a more explicit association of Yahweh's invisibility during the theophany with the prohibition of images than we found in Exodus; this might be a development of the original Mosaic prohibition of images or might represent an association that was present from the beginning but was not part of the strand of the tradition used in Exodus.

And ye came near and stood under the mountain; and the mountain burned with fire unto the midst of heaven, with darkness, clouds, and thick darkness. And Yahweh spake unto you out of the midst of the fire: ye heard the voice of the words, but saw no similitude; only ye heard a voice. . . . Take ye therefore good heed unto yourselves; for ye saw no manner of similitude on the day that Yahweh spoke unto you in Horeb out of the midst of the fire; lest ye corrupt yourselves, and make you a graven image, the similitude of any figure, the likeness of male or female, the likeness of any beast that is on the earth, the likeness of any winged fowl that flieth in the air, the likeness of any thing that creepeth on the ground, the likeness of any fish that is in the waters beneath the earth: and lest thou lift up thine eyes unto heaven, and when thou seest the sun, and the moon, and the stars, even all the host of heaven, shouldest be driven to worship them, and serve them, which Yahweh thy God hath divided unto all nations under the whole heaven [Deuteronomy 4: 11–19].

The suggestion that God divided the stars among other nations for their worship is not consistent with anything hitherto attributed to Moses and looks like a later addition. Star worship is not mentioned earlier in the Mosaic books and seems to have been introduced into Judah through Assyrian influence in the eighth century BC. We know that some sections of this chapter are very late, because it goes on (verses 25–7) to reiterate the prohibition of image worship and to prophesy that the people of Israel, for neglecting this command, will be scattered among the nations, 'and ye shall be left few in number among the heathen, whither Yahweh shall lead you', which indicates that the writer was writing after the exile of 587 BC. There follows a reference to God's forgiveness and an eventual return to the land, which is very reminiscent of parts of Jeremiah and the second Isaiah, in language as well as thought. So at best we are here trying to pick out Mosaic threads in a tapestry woven long after Moses.

The speech continues with further exhortations and injunctions, and in Chapter 5 we have the repetition of the Decalogue that we have discussed in an earlier chapter. Great emphasis is laid on teaching and handing on the tradition to children, Deuteronomy as a whole being organized as what we might call today a text-book of Israelite religion, significantly attributed entirely to Moses. The famous injunction in Chapter 6 to 'love Yahweh thy God with all thine heart, and with all thy soul, and with all thy might' sounds like a post-Mosaic development of the implications of the Mosaic concept of a covenant between Israel and Yahweh. Modern scholarship has seen a connection be-

tween a sentence of this sort and the language used in seventh and eighth century BC treaties, the recently discovered treaty between Esarhaddon, king of Assyria, (680–669 BC) and his eastern vassals being particularly relevant. In these treaties the phrase 'love with all your heart' is used with reference to loyalty to a sovereign. Indeed the structure of Deuteronomy as a whole, with its historical introduction, its exhortations and regulations and its concluding list of blessings for observance and curses for disobedience, has been seen as based on ancient Near Eastern treaty forms.

In Chapter 8 the forty years of wandering in the wilderness are seen as arranged by God 'to humble thee and to prove thee, to know what was in thine heart, whether thou wouldst keep his commandments or no', while the people were allowed to go hungry and then to receive manna in order 'that he might make thee know that man doth not live by bread alone', a much more sophisticated presentation than the simple miracle-story of Exodus 16 and one which must be post-Mosaic. But when in this speech Moses goes on to remind the people that during their forty years in the wilderness 'thy raiment waxed not old upon thee, neither did thy foot swell' it looks as though the writer is making use of a genuinely old tradition, even though it is found nowhere else. The emphasis is on God's fatherly protection of his people, in itself a thoroughly Mosaic idea.

In Chapter 9 we get a splendidly vivid picture, entirely from Moses' point of view, of what happened in Horeb (Sinai) when Moses learned on the mountain of the people's defection:

When I was gone up unto the mount to receive the tables of stone, even the tables of the covenant which Yahweh made with you, then I abode in the mount forty days and forty nights; I neither did eat bread nor drink water: And Yahweh delivered unto me two tables of stone written with the finger of God; and on them was written according to all the words which Yahweh spoke with you in the mount, out of the midst of the fire, in the day of the assembly. And it came to pass at the end of forty days and forty nights, that Yahweh gave me the two tables of stone, even the tables of the covenant. And Yahweh said unto me, Arise, get thee down quickly from hence; for thy people which thou hast brought forth out of Egypt have corrupted themselves; they are quickly turned aside out of the way which I commanded them; they have made them a molten image. Furthermore Yahweh spake unto me, saying, I have seen the people, and, behold, it is a stiffnecked people: Let me alone that I may destroy them, and blot out their name from under heaven: and I will make of thee a nation mightier and greater than

A view from Jebel Katherina.

they. So I turned and came down from the mount, and the mount burned with fire: and the two tables of the covenant were in my two hands. And I looked, and, behold, ye had sinned against Yahweh, and had made you a molten calf: . . . And I took the two tables, and cast them out of my two hands, and brake them before your eyes. And I fell down before Yahweh, as at the first, forty days and forty nights: I did neither eat bread nor drink water, because of all your sins which ye sinned, in doing wickedly in the sight of Yahweh, to provoke him to anger. For I was afraid of the anger and hot displeasure, wherewith Yahweh was wroth against you to destroy you. But Yahweh hearkened unto me at that time also . . . [*Deuteronomy 9: 9–19*].

Some scholars think that some of the details in this lively account were taken from this passage and written into the account of the same incident in Exodus 32. It is of course a conscious literary treatment by a writer who knows what he is doing. But the subject treated – the backsliding of the people so soon after the theophany and before the very Mountain of God itself – must have been in the Moses traditions from the earliest stage. Here it is presented as something to remember and to take warning by. The emphasis throughout Deuteronomy is on warning, exhorting, reminding, so that the people will carry out Yahweh's law. Picturesque ritual details, which so abound in the earlier Mosaic books, disappear. When Moses, continuing his speech, goes on to tell of his making of the ark, it is simply in order to have a receptacle in which to deposit the two tables of stone: there is no mention of its function as Yahweh's throne.

The eloquence of Deuteronomy reminds us of the Prophets rather than of the Moses who has hitherto been presented, and there can be little doubt that the character and ideas of Moses that we find in this book show the influence of post-Mosaic ideas. Yet sometimes we feel that the Deuteronomist sums up, if in his own way, something that must have been at the core of Moses' concept of God, law and people.

And now, Israel, what doth Yahweh thy God require of thee, but to fear Yahweh thy God, to walk in all his ways, and to love him, and to serve Yahweh thy God with all thy heart and with all thy soul. To keep the commandments of Yahweh, and his statutes, which I command thee this day for thy good? Behold, the heaven and the heaven of heavens is Yahweh's thy God, the earth also, with all that therein is. . . . For Yahweh your God is God of gods, and Lord of lords, a great God, a mighty, and a terrible, which regardeth not persons, nor taketh reward: He doth execute the judgment of the fatherless and widow, and loveth the stranger, in giving him food and raiment. Love ye therefore the stranger: for ye were strangers in the land of Egypt [*Deuteronomy 10: 12–19*].

In this eloquent summing up of the matter, the writer has chosen to put into Moses' mouth (a) the association of fearing, obeying, loving and serving God, (b) emphasis on God as creator of the universe, (c) God's power, (d) God's impartiality as a judge with the implication that human judges too should be impartial, (e) God's special concern – and therefore the obligation that Israel too should make it their special concern – with the fatherless and the widow, and (f) the special claims of the stranger (i.e., the resident alien) on Israel's help and understanding. The selection of these points for emphasis may not be a Mosaic selection, but all the points are found in the Mosaic code.

In Chapter 12 of Deuteronomy we get an emphasis on the centralization of worship which is often held to be the characteristic Deuteronomic contribut-tion, for before this there were local sanctuaries throughout Israel and now we are told that there is one place that the Lord will choose, and there and there only people must bring their sacrifices and offerings. This is clearly a late ele-ment, postdating that period of settlement in Palestine when the people wor-shipped at local sanctuaries. An interesting difference between the concept of a single national sanctuary and the concept of the sanctuary we find in the earlier Mosaic records is that in the latter Yahweh is thought actually to come to the sanctuary when he is invoked, but now it is only his *name* that dwells there. Moses, too, as we have seen, was much involved with the implications of God's name, but this is a further development. One consequence of the insistence on a central sanctuary and the prohibition of sacrificing 'in every place that thou seest' is the change in the attitude to slaughtering animals for food. The Mosaic position was that only in ritual sacrifice can domestic animals be killed for food. But with the place of sacrifice not accessible to those who dwelt far from the one allowed sanctuary, it became necessary to change this. Now 'thou mayest kill and eat flesh in all thy gates, whatever thy soul lusteth after, according to the blessing of Yahweh thy God which he hath given thee.' Only the Mosaic prohibition of the eating of the blood remains.

The Mosaic revulsion against any kind of ritual mutilation is emphasized with new specific details. 'Ye are the children of Yahweh your God: ye shall not cut yourselves nor make any baldness between your eyes for the dead.' The Israelites are not called 'children of Yahweh' elsewhere in the Mosaic books, but this phrase may well be a development of the implications of Exodus 4: 22: 'And thou shalt say unto Pharaoh, Thus saith Yahweh, Israel is my son, even my firstborn.' The refusal to participate in any cult of the dead is characteristically Mosaic, and may go back to Moses' own revulsion against the central place of death in Egyptian religion. It is remarkable how, in spite of the omnipresent mystery of death, which would seem to demand a cultic response, 'Israel', in von Rad's words, 'deprived the dead and the grave of every sacral quality. This was a great achievement!' It was an achievement that it is wholly reasonable to attribute to Moses himself.

Further injunctions and commandments follow, often repeating or modifying those we find in Exodus. Sometimes we find a significant change from the Mosaic tradition, as in the transformation of the passover from a domestic feast celebrated by individual families (as Moses saw it) to a pilgrimage feast celebrated at the national sanctuary. Otherwise the three festivals of the year (passover; the feast of weeks, marking the end of the grain harvest; and the feast of tabernacles, marking the end of the vintage) are as in Exodus. The feast of unleavened bread is now seen as combined with the passover (16: 1–3) in what looks like a late addition to the text. Regulations about the festivals are followed by further instructions about justice, and this time a note of secular wisdom combines with the emphasis on divine authority:

Judges and officers shalt thou make thee in all thy gates, which Yahweh thy God giveth thee, throughout thy tribes: and they shall judge the people with just judgment. Thou shalt not wrest judgment, thou shalt not respect persons, neither take a gift: for a gift doth blind the eyes of the wise, and pervert the words of the righteous. That which is altogether just shalt thou follow, that thou mayest live, and inherit the land which Yahweh thy God giveth thee [Deuteronomy 16: 18–20].

We have here the combination of the Mosaic invocation of divine authority, and promise of material blessing for obedience, with the adducing of a human reason for not taking bribes couched in the later language of Proverbs and the so-called 'Wisdom Literature'.

The regulations in Deuteronomy 20 concerning the procedure in going to war are clearly post-Mosaic, but they breathe a spirit of humane concern that it would be pleasant to be able to derive from the Mosaic tradition. A man who has just built a new house, or planted a vineyard and not yet eaten of it, or left behind a betrothed girl whom he has not yet married (and who in his absence may therefore marry someone else!) is relieved of obligation to do military service. So is anyone 'that is fearful and faint-hearted', lest his faint-heartedness infect others. This chapter concludes with a remarkable prohibition against destroying fruit-trees in war: 'When thou shalt besiege a city a long time, in making war against it to take it, thou shalt not destroy the trees thereof by forcing an axe against them: for thou mayest eat of them, and thou shalt not cut them down (for the tree of the field is man's life) to employ them in the siege.' This cannot be paralleled in the earlier Mosaic books, but as it has no parallel either anywhere else in ancient literature, we are perhaps entitled to see it as part of the uniqueness of the Mosaic tradition.

Chapter 22 of Deuteronomy opens with a command to restore 'thy

The plague of lice: from a 12th-century Byzantine Octateuch.

A priest banishes a leper: one of the Mosaic regulations illustrated in the same 12th-century Byzantine Octateuch.

brother's ox or his sheep' if you find it straying. This is a modification of Exodus 23:4: 'If thou meet thine enemy's ox or his ass going astray, thou shalt surely bring it back to him again.' Exodus gives the earlier form, yet it is the more ethically advanced, which shows that ethical ideas do not move in a simple evolutionary straight line. One is tempted to believe that when the Deuteronomist came to that verse of Exodus in his source material he could not believe that the writer really meant to write 'enemy' and so substituted 'brother'. It has been argued that the word translated as 'enemy' really means 'opponent in a lawsuit', since it is in a context devoted to legal procedures, and that the Deuteronomist is simply extending the rule to a man's brother, i.e. any neighbour. But the verse in Exodus is followed immediately by the command to provide help 'if thou see the ass of him that hateth thee lying under his burden', so it does seem as though the Exodus writer is emphasizing the

Soldiers disinfecting their clothes before they leave a city they have sacked: from a 12th-century Byzantine Octateuch.

obligation to assist one's personal enemies in certain cases, and that this was a genuine Mosaic idea.

Amid the repetitions and modification of earlier material, Deuteronomy preserves, in the opening verses of Chapter 23, an ancient set of laws regarding those who are eligible to 'enter the assembly of Yahweh' (i.e. the cultic assembly of adult males meeting on specific occasions of celebration or emergency). Ammonites and Moabites are forbidden, 'because they met you not with bread and with water on the way, when you came forth out of Egypt; and because they hired against thee Balaam . . . to curse thee', but, surprisingly, 'thou shalt not abhor an Edomite, for he is thy brother: thou shalt not abhor an Egyptian, because thou wast a stranger in his land': in the third generation their children can enter the assembly. It is astonishing that the Mosaic tradition preserves a feeling of friendship towards the Egyptians, which must go back to the Joseph tradition and the earlier welcoming of Hebrews in Egypt.

A variety of laws concerning the family and inheritance, loans and debts, lawsuits and quarrels, treatment of servants, provision for the widow, the fatherless and the stranger, weights and measures and other matters are occasionally punctuated by striking affirmations of principle. One such occurs in 24:16: 'The fathers shall not be put to death for the children, neither shall the children be put to death for the fathers: every man shall be put to death for his own sin.' We have already noted the significance of the Mosaic concept of individual responsibility. There is evidence that Israelite practice did not always conform with this principle, and that this verse is an emphatic reassertion of it, the aim being not to emphasize the death penalty (which is here used as the extreme example of punishment) but to emphasize the limitation of guilt to the actual perpetrator of the evil deed.

Chapter 26 of Deuteronomy preserves a formula to be recited by the Israelite when he offers up the firstfruits of his land. It begins with an alliterative statement, *arami obed abi*, 'a wandering Aramean was my father', which sounds like a very ancient formula and apparently refers to the migration of Abraham. (The verb translated as 'wandering' is used for straying animals, which suggests the nomadic background of the Patriarchs.) The statement to be recited then goes on to describe the oppression in Egypt, the deliverance from Egypt by Yahweh and the entry into 'this land, even a land that floweth with milk and honey'. The curious thing is that in this clearly very old formula which summarizes Israel's history from the patriarchal age to the entry into the Promised Land, no mention is made of the giving of the law on Mount Sinai, which was after all the central event of Israel's history. Even if the narrator had forgotten that all this was supposed to be spoken by Moses, how could he have forgotten about Sinai? The supposition has been made that this (and other summaries in the Mosaic books which similarly omit reference to Sinai) belongs to an independent tradition in which the giving of the law on Sinai was unknown. This does not, however, seem a wholly convincing explanation.

The Deuteronomist is approaching the climax of his narrative. Moses reaffirms, in the characteristic Deuteronomic rhetorical style, the people's obligation to Yahweh and his law:

This day Yahweh thy God hath commanded thee to do these statutes and judgments: thou shalt therefore keep and do them with all thine heart, and with all

OPPOSITE Rembrandt's painting of Moses breaking the tables.

OVERLEAF An inlet near Eilat, or Ezion-geber, where the Israelites passed.

thy soul. Thou hast avouched Yahweh this day to be thy God, and to walk in his ways, and to keep his statutes, and his commandments, and his judgments, and to hearken unto his voice. And Yahweh hath avouched thee this day to be his peculiar people, as he hath promised thee, and that thou shouldest keep all his commandments. And to make thee high above all nations which he hath made, in praise, and in name, and in honour; and that thou mayest be a holy people unto Yahweh thy God, as he hath spoken [Deuteronomy 26: 16–19].

Moses commands the elders to carve 'all the words of this law' upon great stones.

There follows a list of curses for those who disobey specific commands, those selected for this purpose being those against making graven or molten images, dishonouring parents, removing a neighbour's landmark, refusing to assist a blind man to find his way, perverting the judgement of the stranger, the fatherless and the widow, committing incest, lying with an animal, slaying a neighbour in secret, taking a bribe to slay an innocent person and failure to confirm the words of this law by obeying them.

The formula here, intended for public recital at a cultic ceremony, is very ancient. Each curse is pronounced in precisely the same ritual way: 'Cursed be he that removeth his neighbour's landmark: and all the people shall say, Amen.' The people's 'amen' signifies their contractual agreement to accept their obligation to Yahweh. The selection of the particular crimes in this list must be Mosaic, though exactly how it is related to the Decalogue and other lists of commandments and prohibitions in the Mosaic books remains a matter of conjecture. It is noteworthy that it is a list of prohibitions only; except for the final general statement, there is no cursing of someone who fails to do what he is commanded to do but the concern is wholly with people who do what they are commanded never to do. The blessings that follow in Chapter 28 are not for obeying any selected commands but for obeying the commandments in general. 'And all these blessings shall come on thee, and overtake thee, if thou shalt hearken unto the voice of Yahweh thy God.' Whereas the curses already cited are not specified – the offender was simply *arur*, afflicted with a curse from God – the blessings are related to specific areas of material prosperity. 'Blessed shalt thou be in the city, and blessed shalt thou be in the field. Blessed shall be the fruit of thy body, and the fruit of thy ground, and the fruit of thy cattle, the increase of thy kine, and the flocks of thy sheep . . .' and so on. But then, just as we may be registering satisfaction that the curses are so few and unspecific while the blessings are richly specific, we come

Michelangelo's famous statue of Moses, part of the tomb of Pope Julius II. It shows him with the legendary horns.

to a second list of curses, this time not linked to particular offences but to non-observance of Yahweh's statutes and commandments in general, and they are not only as specific as the blessings, but much more numerous.

At first the curses precisely match the preceding blessings. 'Cursed shalt thou be in the city, and cursed shalt thou be in the field . . .' and so on. This must be the original form. But other and more horrible details have been added, in the light of the horrors of conquest and exile in 587 BC. The graphic details of disease and drought and conquest and exile clearly date from after the exile, and reveal that mood of almost masochistic self-reproach that we have already diagnosed as characteristic of the Israelites in the Mosaic period. But now it is as though the writer is describing (in the list of blessings) what might have happened if only they had obeyed Yahweh's commands: they would still be living happily and prosperously in their land. But now, because of their sins, they have inherited the curse pronounced on the disobedient. The tone is that of the Prophets and not of Moses, and a similar prophetic tone is found in Chapter 30 in the promise of eventual forgiveness and restoration when Israel returns to Yahweh and heeds his commands. The second list of curses in Deuteronomy and what immediately follows are thus not Mosaic. Nevertheless the return to the promise of blessing for true obedience, with the promise of restored fortunes and the outcasts gathered in 'from all the nations, whither Yahweh thy God hath scattered thee', is an elaboration in the light of later history of the basic idea underlying the Mosaic covenant between Israel and Yahweh.

After this we get a self-contained passage which in its almost pleading reasonableness strikes a note not heard before in the Mosaic books:

For this commandment which I command thee this day, it is not hidden from thee, neither is it far off. It is not in heaven, that thou shouldst say, Who shall go up for us to heaven, and bring it unto us, that we may hear it, and do it? Neither is it beyond the sea, that thou shouldst say, Who shall go over the sea for us, and bring it unto us, that we may hear it, and do it? But the word is very nigh unto thee, in thy mouth, and in thy heart, that thou mayest do it [*Deuteronomy 30: 11–14*].

There is nothing in the Moses traditions that we have identified so far that resembles this. It sounds like a new voice. But the conclusion of Chapter 30, with its reaffirmation that the people have been given the choice 'between life and good and death and evil', its calling on heaven and earth to witness this and the final reference to Yahweh's promise to the Patriarchs, is quite in the spirit of the Mosaic covenant.

We then get another speech from Moses. He announces that he is a hundred and twenty years old 'this day' and that although he is prohibited from cross-ing the Jordan Yahweh will help his people to victory there and Joshua will lead them. The image of Moses as encourager of his people to victory in the Promised Land changes in verse 9 to that of the moral leader whose work as personal mediator between God and his people is now over and who must now write down his law for posterity. 'And Moses wrote this law, and delivered it unto the priests the sons of Levi.' (What exactly is signified by 'this law' is not clear: it is presumably the Book of Deuteronomy up to this point.) Deuteronomy has now abandoned the first person narrative by Moses, and tells us what Moses did and said. Yahweh appeared to him to warn him of his imminent death and to predict that after his death the people will go a-whor-ing after strange gods, to prevent which Moses is to write down and teach to the people the song that appears in Chapter 32.

The Song of Moses (Deuteronomy 32: 1–43) is a remarkable poem written in the characteristic old Hebrew poetic form of parallel clauses, but it clearly derives from a much later period than that of Moses. It seems to have been originally produced independently of Deuteronomy. From its eloquent opening – 'Give ear, O ye heavens, and I will speak; and hear, O earth, the words of my mouth' – through its varied themes of the perfection of Yahweh's work, the injunction to consult the wisdom of earlier generations, Yahweh's great acts done for the children of Israel, Israel's defection and the ensuing judgement, Yahweh's reasons for not punishing Israel indefinitely and Yahweh's return to help and avenge his people, we hear the tone of biblical Wisdom Literature (Job, Proverbs, Ecclesiastes) that developed in a context very different from any situation known to Moses and many hundreds of years after his death. Impressive though the song is, the inquirer after the historical Moses must resolutely exclude it from the relevant evidence.

We return to narrative:

And Yahweh spake unto Moses that selfsame day, saying, Get thee up unto this mountain Abarim, unto mount Nebo, which is in the land of Moab, that is over against Jericho; and behold the land of Canaan, which I give unto the children of Israel for a possession: And die in the mount whither thou goest up, and be gathered unto thy people; as Aaron thy brother died in mount Hor, and was gathered unto his people: Because ye trespassed against me among the children of Israel at the waters of Meribah-Kadesh, in the wilderness of Zin; because ye sanctified me not in the midst of the children of Israel. Yet thou shalt see the land before thee; but thou shalt not go thither unto the land which I give the children of Israel [Deuteronomy 32: 49–52].

This is very largely a repetition of what we have already found in Chapter 27 of Numbers. It is interesting that here, as in Numbers, Moses was not allowed into the Promised Land because of a fault on his part not, as earlier in Deuteronomy, because Yahweh was angry with Moses 'for your [the people's] sake'. The tradition recorded in Numbers and here towards the end of Deuteronomy is surely older than the tradition recorded earlier in Deuteronomy, for it seeks to prove that Moses was punished for a fault, however slight, that he himself had committed, whereas the notion that Yahweh was angry with Moses for the people's sake suggests the doctrine of vicarious atonement which, as we have seen, is not a Mosaic doctrine at all.

There follows another poem, the 'Blessing of Moses' (Deuteronomy 33: 1–29), said to be 'the blessing, wherewith Moses the man of God blessed the children of Israel before his death'. It has some points of similarity with Jacob's blessing of his sons in Genesis 49. But though the poem apparently contains some archaic elements it is not Mosaic, but dates perhaps from the late ninth or early eighth century BC. It is an interruption in the narrative of Deuteronomy 32: 49–52 which we have already quoted. The narrative is taken up in Chapter 34:

And Moses went up from the plains of Moab unto the mountain of Nebo, to the top of Pisgah, that is over against Jericho: and Yahweh showed him all the land of Gilead, unto Dan. And all Naphtali, and the land of Ephraim, and Manasseh, and all the land of Judah, unto the utmost sea. And the south, and the plain of the valley of Jericho, the city of palm trees, unto Zoar. And Yahweh said unto him, This is the land which I sware unto Abraham, unto Isaac, and unto Jacob, saying, I will give it unto thy seed: I have caused thee to see it with thine eyes, but thou shalt not go over thither.

So Moses the servant of Yahweh died there in the land of Moab, according to the word of Yahweh. And he buried him in a valley in the land of Moab, over against Beth-peor: but no man knoweth of his sepulchre unto this day.

And Moses was a hundred and twenty years old when he died: his eye was not dim, nor his natural force abated [Deuteronomy 34: 1–7].

Moses' loneliness is stressed at the moment of death as it was on the crucial occasions of his encounter with the divine. Even his grave remains solitary and unknown. There must have been a tradition attached to a particular locality that associated Moses' grave with that locality, but although the general area remained known the precise place faded from memory. The implication is that that was right: Moses was buried privately by the God he mediated to Israel, and men should not inquire into the divine secret of his lonely grave.

10
Epilogue

The traditional view of the first five books of the Bible – the Pentateuch, i.e. Genesis, Exodus, Leviticus, Numbers and Deuteronomy – is that Moses wrote them under divine inspiration, except for the last eight verses of Deuteronomy, which record his death (though some rabbinical authorities maintained that he wrote those too). Such a view holds the story of Moses' life and achievements recorded in them to be literally true. If one accepts this, then there is nothing more to be said about Moses than what the Bible tells us: his history is there for us to read. But no scholar who has examined with any objectivity the texture of the biblical narrative, studied its internal structure, looked at its linguistic characteristics, and compared it with other ancient Near Eastern literatures as well as with tablets and inscriptions and other evidence unearthed by archaeologists, can doubt that the biblical books that tell us about Moses are related to history in a much more complex, and indeed a much more fascinating, way. We have already said something about the oral traditions that lie behind the different strands of narrative and prescriptions attributed to different writers. What emerges from a study of them is a conviction that between them they perpetuate a memory of critical events, regarded as unique and redemptive by the people of Israel and as constituting their *raison d'être* as a nation. Such a memory cannot be paralleled in the records of other ancient peoples, and it is this that distinguishes the Israelite traditions from those of

Hittites, Amorites, Jebusites and other peoples near or among whom they lived. Martin Noth has defined the main themes embodied in these traditions as the promise to the Patriarchs, the guidance out of Egypt, the revelation at Mount Sinai, the guidance in the wilderness and the guidance into the arable land. In all but the first of these Moses is seen as playing a central part.

Moses is presented in these traditions as a man, and fallible. The experience he underwent alone by the burning bush in Midian led him both to a new conception of God and to a belief in the necessity of bringing the Hebrews out of their Egyptian slavery, but at the same time he is shown as extremely reluctant to undertake that mission himself and as actually arguing persistently with God against God's choice of him for leader. This counterpointing of leadership and meekness, of special divine favour and normal human irritability, seems to be a central part of what was handed down about his character. He spoke, in a sense, face to face with God and brought God's revealed word to his people, but he is not a superman or a saint or an epic hero, or in any way divine or immortal. At the end of the story he dies and he is buried. We are not told that his soul goes marching on or that he took up his place beside God in heaven: such concepts are wholly alien to the Mosaic traditions. But he left behind him laws, given by God, imperatives that were absolute because divinely given. And in spite of the relative secularizing of Mosaic commands that we have seen in Deuteronomy, even there the tradition of divine sanction remains absolutely unshaken.

The Israelites, then, associated their laws with God's irrevocable commands mediated by Moses. Their objective, as God made clear in his covenant, was to enable the people to live in peace, prosperity and stability by obeying them. That is the essence of the Mosaic concept of law. Yet the Mosaic laws are not presented as utilitarian rules to ensure the greatest happiness of the greatest number: God guarantees happiness to the community (rather than to the individual) that obeys them, but this is not because in a naturalistic sequence of cause and effect behaviour in accordance with these laws could be calculated to result in happiness, but because it is God's will that these laws should be carried out and he will favour the community that obeys and punish the community that disobeys. Of course many of the laws are calculated to promote a decent, ordered and satisfying life. But that is not the ostensible reason why God has chosen these laws to promulgate. He has chosen them because they represent his will. The people are not forbidden to eat pig because in a hot climate the flesh of the pig might give the eater trichinosis. The pig is a ritually forbidden animal, repugnant to the cult of Yahweh, probably because the

Moses with the tables of the law, by Champaigne.

wild boar was considered sacred in the Syrian and Phoenician cults. The prohibition of boiling a kid in its mother's milk is not because this offends our humane feelings but probably because such a process was associated with Ugaritic milk spells. But in any case God never gives reasons. The Mosaic commands are presented as divine and therefore by definition absolute.

At the same time some of the most emphatically delivered and repeated Mosaic laws are concerned with social justice and the relief of misery. The reiterated commands to assist the widow, the fatherless and the stranger, the concern with impartial judgement, the interest in the condition of servants, the provisions for alleviating poverty and for not pressing a poor man's debt, these all sound like laws worked out by a compassionate human intelligence in order to further particular social ends. If they are interspersed with cultic commands which to the modern mind may seem irrational or meaningless, they are nonetheless present, and they are emphasized. We must make a distinction between the way the Mosaic tradition presents the laws as requiring unconditional and unreflective obedience because they represent the unchallengeable will of God, and what their historical origin really must be.

Bodies of laws generally develop slowly over a long period of time, but many nations preserve traditions about particular lawgivers who gave new laws or recodified existing laws or in some way gave a significant new impetus to legal theory and practice. Hammurapi of Babylon, Solon of Greece and, in the modern world and in a more limited context, Sir Edward Coke in England were all in their different ways either legal innovators or reinvigorators. In the ancient world a balancing of social need and cultic tradition was achieved by a variety of processes. With respect to Moses it is impossible to say how much of the law associated with his name derives in any significant way from him, how much was modified or codified by him and how much was taken over by him as traditional – or indeed how much traditional material ignored by Moses remained alive and was later absorbed into the Mosaic code. But it was Moses who gave the law a new and special kind of authority by delivering it not only as the commands of God, but as the commands of the God of nature and of history who had by covenant made himself the *melech* (king) of Israel, and whose divine-royal edicts were in an absolutely unique category. To ask such a question as, 'Did the historical Moses really believe that he was delivering to his people laws revealed to him by God?' is to show a certain naiveté about the nature of belief and of tradition. We make distinctions today between conscious role-taking and spontaneous behaviour, and between symbolic ways of presenting truths or facts and the truths or facts themselves, which would not have had any meaning to earlier civilizations. It would be too crude simply to say that we can assume that Moses delivered his laws in the name of Yahweh and in the context of a covenant between Israel and Yahweh because he thought that by getting people to believe this he was guaranteeing that they would obey them. A theophany at Sinai, and Moses' central part in it, became established at an early stage in Israel's consciousness of its own history as the real starting point of their history as a nation. *Something* happened at Sinai in which Moses and lawgiving were involved. By a study of the way in which the traditional accounts of that event were preserved and eventually written down we can try to discern the outlines of the character of the man Moses and of the special nature of his contribution to the laws and customs of his people. Further than that we cannot go.

Can we penetrate through the mists of tradition by means of psycho-analysis? Freud tried to do this with conspicuous lack of success. The best comment on his attempt is Buber's dry sentence: 'That a scholar of so much importance in his own field as Sigmund Freud could permit himself to issue so unscientific a work, based on groundless hypotheses, as his 'Moses and Monotheism' (1939), is regrettable.' A much better informed and interesting attempt to combine psychology, anthropology and ancient history in order to explain the Sinai traditions was made by Theodor Reik in 1959 but, though he has many illuminating things to say by the way, he does not really prove any-thing. His main thesis is 'that a systematic exploration of the biblical report of the Exodus-Sinai events would lead us to the astonishing result that it com-prises the tale of a puberty festival of the Hebrew tribes'. 'At the foundation of the biblical narrative of the Sinai revelation is an historical truth – namely the initiation of the Hebrew tribes into a new religion in the manner of the primi-tive puberty festivals, or the admission into the fraternities of half-civilized people.' The thesis is interestingly argued, but it gets us no nearer to the historical Moses.

The Moses tradition did not come to an end with the traditions recorded in the Pentateuch. Moses entered into Jewish folklore and legend and cabalistic speculation. These traditions take us further and further away from the historical Moses, but they do illuminate the role he was to play in the later imagination of his own people. The humanity and fallibility of Moses were stressed by the rabbis as well as his unique role as lawgiver and confidant of God. Judaism as a religion is historically based on the laws of Moses as inter-preted and amplified by the rabbis. At its centre lies a belief in the revelation at Sinai and Moses' all-important part in it. Yet the religion is not Mosaism as the religion deriving from Jesus Christ is Christianity. Indeed after the rise of

OVERLEAF Moses and Aaron and the ten commandments, by Aaron de Chavez, the first recorded Jewish painter to work in England.

לא תרצח :
No mates .
לא תנאף :
No forniques .
לא תגנב :
No hurtes .
לא תענה -
No atestigues -
לא תחמר -
No cobdicies -

Christianity there seems to have been a conscious intention on the part of the rabbis not to make claims for Moses that could be compared with claims made by Christians for Jesus. While this was fully in accord with the tradition embodied in the Pentateuch, which, as we have noted, showed Moses as a fallible mortal, it nevertheless contributed to the playing down of the part played by Moses in Jewish liturgy and ritual. Thus, while the Pentateuch, the Five Books of Moses, are venerated by orthodox Jews as holy writ and read as well as ceremonially exhibited in the synagogue, Moses is not mentioned once in the ritual for the passover evening, the *Haggadah*. At the same time many fascinating stories about Moses' unique qualities and special relationship with God are preserved in that mass of rabbinical commentary and legend known as the *Aggadah*. One such story tells of Moses' death by the kiss of God on the anniversary of his birth and another tells of his burial by God himself in a grave he had prepared for him at the end of the six days of creation.

In Christian tradition, where so much in the Old Testament is taken as a symbolic prefiguring of the events of the New, Moses is – inevitably, one might almost say – taken to prefigure Jesus, who was the superior and culminating figure. 'For this man was counted worthy of more glory than Moses, inasmuch as he who hath builded the house hath more honour than the house. For every house is builded by some man; but he that built all things is God. And Moses verily was faithful in all his house as a servant, for a testimony of those things which were to be spoken after; but Christ as a son over his own house; whose house are we, if we hold fast the confidence and the rejoicing of the hope firm unto the end' (Hebrews 3: 3–6). Christ's law, which is of the spirit, is contrasted with the Mosaic law, which is of the letter. 'The letter killeth, but the spirit giveth life. But if the ministration of death, written and engraven in stones, was glorious, so that the children of Israel could not steadfastly behold the face of Moses for the glory of his countenance; which glory was to be done away, How shall not the ministration of the spirit be more glorious?' (II Corinthians 3: 6–8). Moses legislated concerning the sacrificing of animals. 'How much more shall the blood of Christ, who through the eternal Spirit offered himself without spot to God, purge your conscience from dead works to serve the living God?' (Hebrews 9: 13–14). There is thus a certain ambivalence in the Christian attitude to Moses, as there is in the Jewish, and the ambivalence in each case derives from the problem of comparison with Christ. For the Christians, Moses and the Mosaic law had to be subordinated to Christ and the new dispensation; for the Jews, any suggestion that Moses was comparable to God or claimed the kind of status Christians

Detail of a Byzantine mosaic showing Christ surrounded by five prophets, Moses at the top right-hand corner: from the Church of the Transfiguration at Jebel Katherina.

attributed to Christ was to be fiercely repudiated, for God was unique and incomparable. We have already noted that the concept of vicarious atonement was quite foreign to Mosaic thought. In this respect Moses was absolutely different from Christ. Yet Moses did have an important role as mediator and intercessor. The idea that a good man was able to intercede with God to achieve God's forgiveness for wrong-doers is well entrenched in the Mosaic books. Indeed the Mosaic idea goes further and suggests that God might be prevailed upon to pardon transgressors because of the merits of their ancestors. This idea of 'original virtue' (as opposed to 'original sin') was to enter deeply into Jewish religious tradition side by side, oddly enough, with the belief that exile for descendants was a just punishment for the sins of ancestors.

Moses figures more prominently in Christian art than one might expect from his place in Christian doctrine. In sculpture a tradition grew up in the Middle Ages of presenting him as a massive bearded figure holding the tables of the law and wearing horns on his forehead. The horns derive from a mis-understanding of the Hebrew verb *karan* ('shone', 'gave forth rays of light') in Exodus 34:35. The Hebrew noun *keren* means either 'horn' or 'ray of light'; Jerome's Latin translation of the Bible, the Vulgate – the authentic biblical text for mediaeval Christendom and for Roman Catholics after the Reforma-tion – understood the verb *karen* as deriving from *keren* meaning 'horn', so instead of understanding the phrase to mean (as it does) 'the skin of Moses' face shone', the Vulgate understood it to mean that Moses' face had acquired horns. These horns can be seen again and again in statues of Moses, from Giovanni Pisanno's early fourteenth-century statue at Siena through Claus Sluter's statue for the great 'Moses fountain' in the cloister of the Carthusian monastery at Dijon a hundred years later, to Michelangelo's gigantic figure in San Pietro in Vincoli, Rome, done between 1513 and 1516. Michelangelo's is the most famous of all statues of Moses. It shows him just as he has come down from Mount Sinai to find the Israelites worshipping the golden calf. He is sitting, draped and heavily bearded, holding the tables of the law in his right hand. His right arm is bare, the left arm is pressed close to his body with his left hand in his lap, his raised head is turned to the left. His expression is one of thunderously majestic indignation.

The events of Moses' life as recorded in the Bible were an obvious source of inspiration for painters. Benozzo Gozzoli's vast series of mural paintings in the Campo Santo at Pisa, begun in 1469, include scenes from the life of Moses (as well as *The Invention of Wine by Noah*, *The Building of the Tower of Babel* and *The Destruction of Sodom*, among many others). The frescoes that decorate the

The head of Moses, with shining rays, a detail from Botticelli's fresco *The Punishment of the Tribe of Korah* in the Sistine Chapel.

Sistine Chapel at the Vatican done by Botticelli and his assistants include one illustrating several episodes in Moses' early life arranged in a single composition and one showing the destruction of Korah, Dathan and Abiram. Among the Luigi Bernadino frescoes in the Brera Gallery, Milan, are scenes from Exodus dating from the early sixteenth century – although by far the bulk of Luigi's biblical paintings illustrate aspects of the New Testament rather than the Old. Tintoretto painted a *Worship of the Golden Calf* for the church of the Madonna dell' Orto, Venice, about 1546 and some years later painted *The Rain of Manna*, *Moses Striking the Rock* and *The Raising of the Serpent in the Wilderness* among his mural paintings for the Scuola di San Rocco, Venice. His contemporary Paolo Veronese twice painted *The Finding of Moses* (in the Hermitage, Leningrad, and the Prado, Madrid). The seventeenth-century French historical and landscape painter Nicolas Poussin produced many paintings dealing with different aspects of Moses' life, including *Moses and the Burning Bush* (in the Copenhagen Museum), *Moses Striking the Rock* (treated many times; all in the Louvre) and *The Dance Around the Golden Calf* (in the National Gallery, London). His Dutch contemporary Rembrandt painted *Moses Breaking the Tables of the Law* (in the Berlin Museum). The most popular Mosaic themes among painters in the Middle Ages, the Renaissance and sometimes later, are the finding of Moses, Moses at the burning bush, crossing the Red Sea, Moses striking the rock, the giving of the law, the breaking of the tables of the law, the raising of the serpent in the wilderness (popular in mediaeval and Renaissance painting as prefiguring the raising of the cross, just as Moses at the burning bush was taken to prefigure the annunciation and the virgin birth). Some of these themes are treated in illuminated manuscripts as well as in paintings. Scenes from Exodus are also found in Jewish art, in illustrated and illuminated *Haggadot* (passover eve service books). The most famous of these, the fourteenth-century Sarajevo *Haggadah*, shows the whole of biblical history from the creation to the death of Moses in sixty-nine illuminated panels on thirty-four leaves. The pictures include the finding of Moses, Moses and his flock at the burning bush, Moses and Aaron at Pharaoh's court, the ten plagues, the exodus, the crossing of the Red Sea, Moses on Sinai with the tables of the law, Moses giving his final blessing to the people, Moses laying his hands on Joshua at the foot of Mount Nebo before ascending the mountain to die. The old Jewish tradition of illustrated *Haggadot* has been revived and modernized in our time by Ben Shahn (*Ben Shahn's Haggadah*, 1965).

The first significant entry of Moses into European literature is in those mediaeval cycles of plays crudely dramatizing biblical history from the crea-

The plagues of Egypt, illustrated in the *Golden Haggadah*, one of the best known of the Haggadahs.

tion to the last judgement, known as miracle plays. Those that deal with Old Testament themes make consistent efforts to present them in New Testament clothing, as it were, not only seeing Old Testament characters and events as prefiguring New Testament characters and events but actually putting Christian language into the mouths of their Old Testament characters. (This is more often simple naiveté than any deliberate attempt to show parallels.) For example, in the play on the murder of Abel in the Townley Cycle, Cain swears by Christ, while Noah in the Wakefield Cycle appeals for help to the Trinity in building the ark and does so 'in nomine patris et filii et spiritus sancti'. The Moses of mediaeval religious drama, both in England and on the Continent, is thus very much a mediaeval Christian character. At the same time, this kind of anachronism is part of the sense of lively contemporaneity with which the mediaeval imagination recreated the biblical story. Here, for example, is 'Moyses' speaking to the people in the play *Balaam and Balak*, the fifth in the Chester Cycle:

> You, Gods folke of Israell,
> Hearkens to me that loven heale.
> God bade, you sholde doe everye deale
> As that I shall saye:
> Six dayes boldelye worches all,
> The seaventh, Sabaoth you shall call:
> That daye, for ought that may befall,
> Hallowed shal be for aye.

Pharaoh, the seventh play in the Wakefield Cycle, gives a series of vividly presented incidents illustrating Moses' life from the scene at the burning bush to the victory at the Red Sea (when the drowning Pharaoh calls on Mohammed for help!).

Post-mediaeval European literature at first showed little interest in Moses even when European sculptors and painters were employing Mosaic themes. In England by the eighteenth century the name suggested to most people a Jewish old-clothes dealer or money-lender rather than the Old Testament hero: 'Moses' is the name Sheridan gives to the money-lender in *The School for Scandal* (1777). Hannah More's *Moses in the Bulrushes*, one of her *Sacred Dramas* (1782), hardly redressed the balance: its heavy rhetorical didacticism (she informed the reader that she 'rather aspired after Moral Instruction than the purity of Dramatic Composition'), though reasonably popular for a while in her own time, has not worn well. Moses fared better in music in eighteenth-

An ornate 15th-century book cover showing Moses and Aaron and, between them, the rod surmounted by the brazen serpent.

century England. Handel's *Israel in Egypt* (1738: libretto by Charles Jennens) is one of the most impressive of his oratorios on biblical themes, of which there are more than a dozen.

The romantic movement brought a new kind of literary interest in Moses. He was now seen as a lonely heroic figure wearing himself out in the service of a people that does not understand him. French romanticism was especially receptive to this view: Alfred de Vigny's *Moïse* (1822), emphasizing the necessary solitude of genius, presents Moses on Mount Nebo as a tragic figure, weary and alone, asking God to release him from his burdensome task. Chateaubriand's verse tragedy *Moïse* (1836) also presents the romantic Moses. Different attitudes have emerged in the twentieth century. Rainer Maria Rilke's quite short lyric 'Der Tod Moses' ('The Death of Moses', 1922) describes the incredible encounter between God and Moses to conclude (in J. B. Leishmann's translation):

ABOVE Moses crossing the Red Sea: a stained-glass window from the 13th-century basilica of St Denis, Paris.

OPPOSITE A page from the Codex Landau showing the crossing of the Red Sea.

Scenes from the life of Moses, from Ghiberti's famous Gates of Paradise, the bronze doors to the baptistery, Florence.

> Then slowly the aged
> God bowed down his aged face to the aged
> mortal. Withdrew him out of himself in kisses
> into his older age. And with hands of creation
> swiftly remounted the mountain, until it amounted
> to nothing more than the others, lightly surmounting
> human conjecture.

Very different in tone is the verse play *Moses* (1916), by the Anglo-Jewish poet Isaac Rosenberg who was killed in the First World War at the age of twenty-seven. It is no more than a fragment in two scenes, the first vividly presenting the conflicts in Moses' own mind at the time when he is still regarded by Pharaoh as his son and the second, which ends with Moses' slaying of the Egyptian overseer, fiercely enacting Moses' complex relationship with both oppressed and oppressor. A simpler view of Moses, as the giver of the Ten

Commandments to the whole of western civilization, is presented in his eight-line lyric, 'The Jew':

> Moses, from whose loins I sprung,
> Lit by a lamp in his blood
> Ten immutable rules, a moon
> For mutable lampless men. . . .

Rosenberg asks why, since all western peoples 'keep tide to the moon of Moses', should then sneer at his descendant?

At the Law Students' Debating Society of University College, Dublin, the patriotic Irish barrister and orator John F. Taylor made a famous speech on 24 October 1901, in which he defended the study of the Irish language against the cultural claims of English by drawing an analogy between Moses and the Irish patriots. James Joyce, who heard the speech, later gave his version of it in *Ulysses* (1922): it is one of the most remarkable references to Moses in literature:

Mr chairman, ladies and gentlemen: Great was my admiration in listening to the remarks addressed to the youth of Ireland a moment ago by my learned friend. It seemed to me that I had been transplanted into a country far away from this country, into an age remote from this age, that I stood in ancient Egypt and that I was listening to a speech of some highpriest of that land addressed to the youthful Moses. . . .

– Why will you Jews not accept our culture, our religion and our language? You are a tribe of nomad herdsmen; we are a mighty people. You have no cities nor no wealth: our cities are hives of humanity and our galleys, trireme and quadrireme, laden with all manner merchandise furrow the waters of the known globe. You have but emerged from primitive conditions: we have a literature, a priesthood, an agelong history and a policy.

– You pray to a local and obscure idol: our temples, majestic and mysterious, are the abodes of Isis and Osiris, of Horus and Ammon and Ra. Yours serfdom, awe and humbleness: ours thunder and the seas. Israel is weak and few are her children: Egypt is an host and terrible are her arms. Vagrants and daylabourers are you called: the world trembles at our name.

– But, ladies and gentlemen, had the youthful Moses listened to and accepted that view of life, had he bowed his head and bowed his will and bowed his spirit before that arrogant admonition he would never have brought the chosen people out of the house of bondage nor followed the

OVERLEAF Lippi's painting of the worship of the golden calf.

253

pillar of the cloud by day. He would never have spoken with the Eternal amid lightnings on Sinai's mountaintop nor ever have come down with the light of inspiration shining in his countenance and bearing in his arms the tables of the law, graven in the language of the outlaw.

Though there are errors and anachronisms in this account (Moses was no longer young when he renounced his Egyptian affiliation and discovered his identity with his fellow Hebrews; the term 'Jews' for Hebrews or Israelites was quite unknown at this period; etc.) it is a brilliant evocation of the contrast between Hebrew and Egyptian culture as it must have appeared to the Egyptians – and indeed to many Hebrews – at the time of the exodus, and, placed at a significant point fairly early in *Ulysses* (the seventh or 'Aeolus' episode) it reverberates through the rest of the book to give a new dimension to the fallibilities, humilations and frustrations of its Irish-Jewish hero, Leopold Bloom.

In America Lawrence Langner's play *Moses* (1924) uses both Freud and Marx to present Moses as the primitive puritan moralist who sees law as opposed to beauty, which is championed by Miriam. The worship of the golden calf is defended by Miriam as a finer way of worshipping than killing animals in sacrifice: it represents art and imagination rather than stark edicts demanding obedience. One can see the influence of G. B. Shaw in this deliberate reversal of the traditional view which sees Moses as grand but wrong and Miriam as the possessor of true insight. In England, Christopher Fry's tragedy *The Firstborn*, performed at the second Edinburgh Festival in 1948, presents Moses initially as a brilliantly successful former general of Pharaoh's now desperately needed by him – and this gives Moses a bargaining weapon which eventually leads to the exodus. Fry differs from Langner in that he does not remove the divine and miraculous elements. Moses' own enormous powers of leadership and understanding produce divine intervention (rather as sheer will-power changes the terms of human existence in Shaw's *Back to Methuselah*) and enable him to liberate his people. At the same time the violence and cruelty involved in successful liberation appals Moses, who was not prepared for the actualities of divine retribution. The death of Pharaoh's first-born, whom he loved, deeply moves him:

> I do not know why the necessity of God
> Should feed on grief; but it seems so. And to know it
> Is not to grieve less, but to see grief grow big
> With what has died.

Moses is trapped between his ideals and the harsh practicalities involved in carrying them out. This is a not unjustifiable reading of the story as it is given to us in the biblical text.

The story of Moses has inspired a large number of oratorios, cantatas and even operas. They include Vivaldi's oratorio *Moyses Deus Pharaonis* (1714), of which however only the libretto has survived, Handel's *Israel and Egypt* (already referred to), Carl Phillipp Emanuel Bach's oratorio *Die Israeliten in der Wueste* (*The Israelites in the Wilderness*, 1755), Rossini's opera *Mosé in Egitto* (*Moses in Egypt*, 1818), Saint-Saens' cantata (with text by Victor Hugo) *Moïse sauvé des eaux* (*Moses saved from the waters*), Anton Rubenstein's oratorio *Moses* (1892), and Schoenberg's opera *Moses and Aaron*, left unfinished at his death in 1951 but successfully produced in its unfinished form. Schoenberg wrote his own libretto, and the resulting interaction of words and music is uniquely powerful.

Moses and Aaron is the most profound of all modern interpretations of Moses in art. The contrast between the eloquent Aaron, who finds no difficulty in articulating his ideas about God and his choice of Israel, and the inarticulate Moses whose tragedy is that his concept of God is beyond easy formulation and his attempts to formulate it are doomed to misunderstanding, underlies everything that happens in the opera. God needs Aaron because Moses' understanding is too profound for human comprehension; yet Aaron, in making Moses' message intelligible, is bound to distort it. The scene of the worshipping of the golden calf, with which Act II opens, is astonishing in its power and virtuosity. Moses descends with the two tables to find the orgy in progress, and banishes the golden calf at a glance: 'Begone, you that are the image of the fact that what is measureless cannot be bounded in an image.' The ensuing dialogue between Moses and Aaron shows Aaron, as always, plausible, persuasive, understanding of ordinary human needs: the people need an image if they are to achieve any understanding of Moses' sublime notions, notions which, put abstractly, cannot be understood by men. Moses can find no answer; he smashes the tables of the law in bitter frustration; the people continue their march across the stage led by the pillar of fire, and it looks as though Aaron was right. Moses, left alone on the stage, agonizes over the consequences of the paradox that to express the inexpressible is to destroy its true meaning. 'O word, thou word that I lack,' he cries, sinking baffled and exhausted to the ground. And there, at the end of Act II, the unfinished opera breaks off. But its profound and disturbing meaning – a meaning, further, that is wholly compatible with the biblical text – has already been communicated.

At the other extreme from Schoenberg, there is the negro spiritual, which has perpetuated a memory of Moses the liberator in a 'simple, sensuous and passionate' medium appreciated all over the world. For one person who has responded to the intricate and complex patterns of Schoenberg's music, so intimately related to the powerful words, there must be many millions who have been moved by the simple melodic line and the unsophisticated expressive words of

> When Israel was in Egypt land
>   (Let my people go)
> Oppressed so hard they could not stand
>   (Let my people go) . . .

> Go down, Moses,
> 'Way down in Egypt land:
> Tell ole Pharaoh
> To let my people go.

As for Moses in the popular imagination, he is at the same time the biblical hero and the bearer of an archetypal Jewish name often employed for comic or satiric effect. Isaac Watts introduced him into the hymnal in the eighteenth century:

> Could we but climb where Moses stood,
> And view the landskip o'er,
> Nor Jordan's stream, nor death's cold flood,
> Should fright us from the shore.

For generations schoolboys have asked each other: 'Where was Moses when the light went out?' and replied, 'Under the bed, looking for the matches.' Thus he moved easily from the sublime to the ridiculous, a fate shared by many great names. Moses shares with God and Jesus Christ the distinction of being invoked in oaths and exclamations. When he legislated against taking the name of the Lord in vain, he cannot have imagined how his would have been used in the remote future. The Oxford English Dictionary gives 1855 as the first recorded use of 'Holy Moses!' 'as an oath or expletive'. But Moses, that meek man, would have repudiated any exclusive claim to that adjective: all the people, he said, should be holy.

Select Bibliography

W. F. Albright, *The Biblical Period from Abraham to Ezra* (Oxford 1952).

W. F. Albright, *From the Stone Age to Christianity*, 2nd ed. (Baltimore 1946).

W. F. Albright, *New Horizons in Biblical Research* (London 1966).

Cyril Aldred, *Akhenaten, Pharaoh of Egypt* (London 1968).

John Bright, *A History of Israel*, 2nd ed. (London 1972).

Martin Buber, *Kingship of God* (New York 1972).

Martin Buber, *Moses* (Oxford 1946).

T. H. Gaster, *Myth, Legend and Custom in the Old Testament* (London 1969).

T. H. Gaster, *Thespis: Ritual, Myth and Drama in the Ancient Near East* (New York 1950).

John Gray, *Archaeology and the Old Testament World* (London 1962).

A. Heidel, *The Gilgamesh Epic and Old Testament Parallels* (Chicago and London 1963).

H. G. May (ed.), *Oxford Bible Atlas*, 2nd ed. (London 1974).

Martin Noth, *A History of Pentateuchal Traditions*, trans. B. W. Anderson (Englewood Cliffs 1972).

Martin Noth, *Exodus, A Commentary*, trans. J. S. Bodwen (London 1962).

H. M. Orlinsky, *Ancient Israel*, 2nd ed. (Ithaca, N.Y. 1960).

J. B. Pritchard (ed.), *Ancient Near Eastern Texts Relating to the Old Testament*, 3rd ed. (Princeton 1969).

Theodor Reik, *Mystery on the Mountain* (New York 1959).

H. H. Rowley, *From Joseph to Joshua* (London 1950).

H. H. Rowley, *From Moses to Qumran* (London 1963).

H. H. Rowley (ed.), *The Old Testament and Modern Study* (Oxford 1951).

W. K. Simpson (ed.), *The Literature of Ancient Egypt* (London and New York 1972).

Gerhard von Rad, *Deuteronomy, A Commentary*, trans. Dorothea Barton (London 1966).

J. A. Wilson, *The Burden of Egypt* (Chicago 1951).

The Authorized Version of the Bible.

J. H. Hertz (ed.), *The Pentateuch and Haftorahs: Hebrew Text, English Translation and Commentary*, 5 vols (London 1929–36).

B. Kittel (ed.), *Biblia Hebraica*, 3rd ed. (Stuttgart 1937). (Authoritative text of the Hebrew Bible.)

Encyclopaedia Judaica, 16 vols (Jerusalem 1972).

Acknowledgements

The author and publisher would like to thank the following museums, institutions and photographers for supplying the illustrations reproduced on the pages listed below:

A–Z Botanical Collections Ltd 102; Bildarchiv Foto Marburg 22, 87, 104, 108, 183, 184; British Museum 83, *120*, *148*, 245; Camera Press Ltd 18, 21 (top), 174, 213, 241; A.C.Cooper, *38–9*; Courtauld Institute of Art 221, 222, 223; Arnold Fawcus and the executors of Ben Shahn *197*; John Freeman 83, *120*, 245; Glyptotek Ny Carlsberg 130; Guidhall Library *38–9*; Sonia Halliday 17, 33, *40*, 102 (bottom), 248; David Harris 91, 97, 98, 100, 101, *117*, 142–3, 155, 165, 166, 205, 216, *226–7*; Michael Holford Library *37*; Israel Museum and Department of Antiquities and Museums, Ministry of Education 32, 188; Mansell Collection 25, 26 (top and bottom right), 35, 44, 48, 74, 80–1, 113, 193, 246, 252–3; National Gallery 12–13, 43, 132–3, 160–1, 190–1; Pierpont Morgan Library 131; Radio Times Hulton Picture Library 14, 15, 17, 21 (bottom), 29, 42, 47, 58, 61, 70, 71, 72, 76, 77, 94, 122, 137, 158, 163, 180, 206, 234, 238–9, 242; Rheinisches Bildarchiv 138; Scala 65, *66–7*, *68*, 88–9, *118–19*, *145*, *146–7*, *178–9*, *198–9*, *200*, 210–11, *228*, 249, 250; Ronald Sheridan 99, 107, 168–9, 171; Staatliche Museen, Berlin *225*, Uni Dia Verlag 31; University of Pennsylvania 22 (top left); Victoria and Albert Museum 62 (bottom), 73, 129; H.Roger Viollet 62 (top), 114.

Numerals in italics indicate colour illustrations.

Picture research by Pat Hodgson.
The maps on pages 10, 84 and 177 were drawn by Jennifer Johnston.

Index